Blazing Saddles

Some books by James Clarke

NATURAL HISTORY
Man is the Prey (New York and London)
Focus on Fauna (with John Pitts)
Our Fragile Land
The Environmental Crisis
Survival Guide to the Outdoors
Mountain Odyssey (with David Coulson)
Roof of Africa (New York) (with David Coulson)
Sabi Sabi
Back to Earth
Coming back to Earth

HISTORY
Like it Was
An Extraodinary 20th Century

HUMOUR
The Bedside Star (edited)
Back to Bed (edited)
Bedtime Again (edited)
The Yellow Six
The Search for the Great South African Limerick
S*x for the Extremely Shy
Laugh, the Beloved Country (with Harvey Tyson)
Enclosed, Please Find
Great South African Limericks
Funny Side of Golf
Clarke on Your Stoep

Blazing Saddles

The true story behind the *Tours de Farce*

James Clarke

Interruptions by Harvey Tyson (Ed)

Drawings by Julie Clarke-Havemann

JONATHAN BALL PUBLISHERS
JOHANNESBURG & CAPE TOWN

This book is dedicated to those we leave behind each year –
Arlene, Pat, Lenka, Joanne and Elizabeth and
to Peter's daughters, Helen and Julia.
(They'd never be able to keep up with us anyway)

Published in 2007 by
JONATHAN BALL PUBLISHERS (PTY) LTD
PO Box 33977
Jeppestown
2043

ISBN-13: 978-1-86842-267-8
ISBN-10: 1-86842-267-4

Front cover photograph by Peter Sullivan
Back cover photogrph by Alan Calenborne
Cover design by Flame Design, Cape Town
Typesetting and reproduction of text and picture sections by
Triple M Design & Advertising
Set in 11/13.5pt Photina MT STD
Printed and bound by
Paarl Print, Cape Town

Acknowledgements

The annual *Tour de Farce* involves four editors, a newspaper columnist and a retired company director and I have placed them in order of the oldest to the youngest to avoid unseemly bickering:

Harvey Tyson – author, travel writer and keen golfer. Harvey was one of the longest-serving editors of *The Star* in Johannesburg (1974-1990). He was born to the sound of roaring lions (Johannesburg Zoo was round the corner). Following a decade at Kingswood College, Grahamstown, he 'passed out of Rhodes University after a year to join the university of life'. He was a journalist for 50 years and edited *The Star* through the bitterest of the apartheid years. He has authored several books, serious and humorous. He continues to travel extensively although he is semi-retired in Hermanus, Cape, where he keeps finding golf balls.

Rex Gibson – former editor of the *Rand Daily Mail* and the *Sunday Express*. He retired in the 1990s as deputy editor-in-chief of *The Star*. He was born in Salisbury, Rhodesia (now Harare, Zimbabwe) and is the author of some very serious books. Now retired to Hermanus where he keeps losing golf balls.

James Clarke – the **L*E*A*D*E*R** of the *Tour de Farce* (I say this with my customary and widely admired humility). I am a columnist on

The Star in Johannesburg. I was born in London and during World War II, as a Boy Scout, collected silver paper from chocolate bars for recycling into Spitfires and Hurricanes, enabling the RAF to sweep the Luftwaffe from British skies and for which I was awarded a quite large certificate.

Alan Calenborne – a retired CEO of an international company that designed and operated parking facilities and toll roads in South Africa, Asia and Europe. Born in Pietermaritzburg, a keen sportsman (mainly rugby and tennis) who, after university, spent 18 months lumber jacking in British Columbia and the Yukon. He was among the 'Maritzburg Mafia' – zoologists and biologists who graduated from Natal University in the 1960s and eventually held key positions in conservation throughout Africa. Mostly by default he became our official photographer. Currently, he enjoys spending as much time as possible outdoors while waiting patiently for the world to recognise his photographic genius.

Richard Steyn – born in Cape Town, educated at Rondebosch Boys' High School and the University of Stellenbosch, he was an attorney in Durban and London before giving up law to edit the *Natal Witness* for many years; was awarded a Nieman Fellowship (to Harvard); captained Natal at rugby and played cricket for Western Province. He moved up to Johannesburg to succeed Harvey as editor-in-chief of *The Star*. Now in publishing, he produces the annual *South African Travel Guide* and the year book, *South Africa at a Glance*. His website, www.satravelguide.com includes the *Tour de Farce's* website.

Peter Sullivan – current group editor-in-chief of Independent Newspapers which includes *The Star*. Born in Bloemfontein, he studied at Wits, Unisa, the University of Cape Town and the Poynter Institute in America. He succeeded Richard Steyn as editor of *The Star*. A tireless traveller he annually attends the World Economic Forum at Davos, Switzerland; serves on international bodies and, at the request of George Soros, he created the Open Society Foundation of South Africa.

I must add that Peter joined us only after *Tour de Farce II* in 2004. That year an old friend, **Lawton Christiane**, dropped out of our team because of clashing travel commitments. Lawton is a retired manufacturer who, years ago, resigned from a big American corporation to go off on his own to successfully compete with them. It was Lawton who, by a chance remark over a lunch, triggered this whole crazy idea.

I have a lot of people to thank especially Harvey Tyson. Our association goes back almost 50 years when I spent a brief period on the *Daily News* in Durban. Harvey was my editor on *The Star* for 17 years during which I was writing, with his encouragement, grown-up stuff about the environment and town and regional planning. He and I co-authored *Laugh, the Beloved Country* in 2003. He very sportingly agreed to critically read and rough edit the manuscript of *Blazing Saddles* – for nothing – although, I suspect, he really wanted to make sure I didn't defame him. I invited him to add his own comments here and there in the book if he thought I'd been remiss or wrong. The real editor was Valda Strauss who was by far the sweetest editor I have ever been corrected by.

As usual I would like to thank my daughter Julie for her drawings and her husband Glenn Havemann. I thank Jeremy Boraine and Francine Blum of Jonathan Ball Publishers and I am particularly grateful to the designer of this book, Kevin Shenton of Triple M Design, Johannesburg who was such a great pleasure to work with.

Then, of course, I owe a great deal to the rest of my companions – Rex for his quiet wisdom and consistent encouragement with this book; Richard for his many useful suggestions; Alan for his photographs; and Peter for his forbearance when, in the last half of this book, I rag him about his name-dropping. And I thank Lawton for the idea of cycling as a way to health and in order to live forever. Live forever? Well, so far so good.

Alan's name should be writ large because most of the photographs in this book are his. The exceptions being the pictures of Ireland which are all by Peter Sullivan (Alan missed that particular trip through illness) and one or two pictures of the Danube leg taken by Lawton.

I must thank my wife (or go without supper) for putting up with my long absences in my study crouched over my PC. In fact my companions have all asked me to thank their wives and partners but I have suggested this would be a cheapskate way for them to show gratitude and that they should rather each go out and buy their partners something really expensive.

And there are the readers of my column, *Stoep Talk*, who helped with advice and who year after year generously provide me with so many thoughts, ideas and laughs: Prof John Earl (ex Wits geographer), Prof Mike Bruton (an ichthyologist turned 'cycologist'), Gus Ferguson (pharmacist, long-distance cyclist and the country's leading writer of comic verse), Chris Moerdyk, Adrian Steed, Alan Busuttil, Victor Strugo, Don Bryant, Nigel Fox, Prof Tim Couzens (even though he has never learned to ride a bike), Sue Stricker of The Skittles cycling group, Ethel Ross who, after our return from the Danube, advised, 'Next year try one of the rivers in France.' We did and it was marvellous.

I thank my long-time colleague, travel editor Carol Lazar whose headline over a *Tour de Farce* photograph inspired the title of this book. And that tireless travel writer, Winnie Graham of *The Star.* Lola Futurman taught three of us, gratis, some basic French.

Serena Cartwright helped us enormously – especially in her capacity as South African representative for Cycling of Softies in the UK; Crown Blue Line and Connoisseur (who arrange boats on the Canal du Midi and elsewhere) and ATG Oxford. In fact she became a friend. We are also grateful to Susi Madron in Manchester, the propretor of Cycling for Softies. There's Edwin Swan, Christine Waring and Elmarie Hall at VisitBritain's offices in Johannesburg who just couldn't do enough for us; Inge Dobihal of the Austria Connection who helped so much with the first *Tour de Farce*; Leigh Eastwood of British Airways for her amazing (and I mean amazing) patience; Helen Fraser of Tourism Ireland (another friend) and Shireen Davids (Peter's secretary); Jacci Babich of the *Sandton Chronicle*, Wendy Carter of Capital Sport, UK who was so generous with her time in helping us plot a course down the Thames, and 'African Cycle Safari' promoter Liz Szabo and her business partner Chris Murray with whom we shared many hilarious hours.

When it comes to cycling lore our chief advisers were Alan van Heerden, and Andrew Mclean (the latter being CEO of Cycle Lab). Andrew's bright yellow shirts became our trademark for a long time. Vincent Stevens of Omnico in Randburg presented each of us with an ultra-lightweight silver Bell helmet (the best you can buy) – a helmet that was to save my coiffeur when I took a bad spill in Ireland.

James Clarke
Johannesburg

*'I can't ride on the flat,
I can't ride in the mountains and I can't do sprints.
I'm the complete all-rounder.'*

[Winner of the Lanterne Rouge (red lantern) –
the trophy that goes to the man who finishes last in the *Tour de France.*]

Foreword

Warning

What is truth? When half a column of ex-newspaper editors debate this deeply philosophical, quintessentially existential and boring question – there is no answer. But be warned that the contents of this book represent only one version of the truth. There are at least five of us with other versions clamouring to contradict it.

However, this is as good a version as you are going to find. It is, I have to confess, the best. It is what newspapers call 'a no-holds-barred exposé of behind-the-scenes intrigue' involving the largely innocent members of the six-man *Tour de Farce* team. It is indeed a story filled with farce, yet within its telling there is suspense, horror, satire, adventure, comedy and suffering. But be warned again, there is little love interest – and no true romance. (Unless you count a reference in this studious work to Saint Emilion, who spent years sleeping on a cold slab of rock to demonstrate his love for the Virgin Mary.)

Hard facts are what make these wheels go round. You will learn, in an instant, such things as why democracy doesn't work, why mankind's gift of language is faltering, and what is wrong with Europe's culture. You will find useful information on how to ride a bicycle while waving at gaping bystanders. And tips on what not to do when totally lost. There's even a recipe for *fustolt lazac*, a Hungarian compilation filled with simple complexities.

There is one secret hidden in this book which, in the noble cause of transparency, I cannot help but reveal. It is this: behind the façade of the self-styled L*E*A*D*E*R of the *Tour de Farce* lurks a modest, dissembling, astonishing fellow. It would be hard to find another in the world who could complete the variety of expeditions involving the recalcitrant members he has successfully 'led' all this century. He has put together, half a dozen times, a group of five adventurers who are generous to a fault. They are adventurers in the sense that they will go anywhere and drink almost anything. They are generous to a serious fault in that they will give, but seldom take. At least in the matter of instructions and advice, they will wholeheartedly give decisions and advice, and decline to take any. James Clarke knows that each is exasperatingly individualistic and filled with self-assured opinions. So he bumbles along pretending to know nothing ... and lets them argue among themselves as they 'lead' him to where he wants to go. He is a past master dodderer in a team of carefully selected dodderers. His doddering is brilliant and genuine, and admired by all. That's the only reason I can find to explain the fact that the *Tour de Farce* has so far completed five expeditions into darkest Europe – though not necessarily on the planned route. None would ride with any other 'leader'.

I shall not reveal what other secrets are unveiled, except to say that this is an unfinished mystery. The *Tour de Farce's* most mature member is a mere 78 years old and 20 years older than the youngest dodderer in the team – so this is not the end of the story. It may be only the beginning. And these things come in cycles.

Harvey Tyson – Ed

Chapter One

We were old enough to have known better. Well, all right, Richard was only 58 but the rest of us were certainly old enough. Here we were, six grown men whose ages averaged 67, about to set out on a nearly 1 000km cycle ride down the River Danube. Perhaps it was nearer 900km but I am speaking of genuine kilometres, the sort they have in France. We planned to follow the Danube from Passau in Germany, across Austria, across the tip of Slovakia and into Hungary, and on as far as Budapest.

I had been led to believe the ride would be downhill all the way.

'Anyway it's logical,' I explained to my prospective though hesitant companions. 'River courses are famous for running downhill; *ipso fatso*, as they say in my local cake shop, the cycle track along it must do something similar.'

It was the first of many assumptions that proved to be not terribly accurate.

The upshot of it all was that a few months later the six of us found ourselves inside a bicycle-hire depot on the periphery of the medieval town of Passau inspecting the Austrian-made trek bikes we were about to sit astride for the next couple of weeks. Harvey observed that picking the right bike was more important than picking a mate.

'It must,' he said, 'be a bicycle of docile but steadfast character with gentle saddle and – vitally important – of precise and peculiar height to suit the rider.' In other words it was no good anybody trying to adjust a bike that was suitable for Richard, who is almost two metres tall, for Rex or me who, even standing on soapboxes, are considerably shorter.

We minutely inspected our bikes; we rang their bells, listening to them intently and professionally as if tuning a harp. We squeezed the tyres and clicked the gears. There were 21 of them.

'I've never seen so many gears,' muttered Rex who is inclined to growl to himself into his clipped beard which, like his close-cropped hair, is silver.

'What's that about "so many years"?' asked Harvey who, like me, is somewhat deaf. Harvey, the oldest of us, hardly has a grey hair in the mop that sometimes hangs over his forehead, and has the stamina of a long-distance runner.

'Gears, gears,' repeated Rex whose low-resonance voice means he has to repeat practically everything he says no matter to whom he is speaking.

'Every bike these days has at least 21,' said Lawton who, perhaps fortunately, is inclined to speak loudly and who knows a lot about bikes. My other four companions were as inexperienced as I – none of us had seriously cycled since our first childhood.

The fellow in charge of the cycle depot came over and asked us with more anxiety in his voice than I thought was warranted, 'Are you sure you're going to be all right?' We were, I suppose, an odd-looking group. We ranged from very tall – Richard and Alan – to short and stocky – Rex and me. The other two, Harvey and Lawton, were more athletic and carried less fat between them than an acid drop. We were attired in form-fitting canary-yellow cycling shirts emblazoned with the words 'Cycle Lab' – the name of the Johannesburg cycle firm that had fitted us out – and blue bum-hugging Lycra cycling shorts. Yet, despite our professional appearance, the cycle-hire man looked genuinely concerned. We thought afterwards that he might have been misled by the word 'Lab' on our shirts. Maybe he thought we were part of some heartless geriatric experiment.

One by one we mounted our bikes and wobbled out of the shed onto the small cobbled square outside Passau's *bahnhof*. It was quiet in the station forecourt where we tested our bikes, but we realised that traversing Passau town centre would be something else entirely. We were going to have to cycle clean through it in peak traffic.

We had spent the previous day walking round the medieval section of Passau which is set on a wedge of land between the rivers Danube and Inn. The river Ilz enters from the north. The town and great water junction nestles between steep forested hills. Its denizens have traditionally made fine swords that, over the centuries, have done a lot to trim the population of Central Europe.

It would have been sensible for us to have spent the previous evening carbo-loading and having an early night but, without our wives around to say, 'Don't you think you've had enough?' we had recklessly spent it wining and dining and offering each other toasts – a toast to our cycling success; a toast to our boundless courage; a toast to our good health; a toast to our wives back home (God bless them); and to many other worthy things all now a little hazy.

The expedition had, more by accident than design, been labelled, the *'Tour de Farce'*, but now, as we circled outside the *bahnhof*, the whole enterprise had suddenly become very serious and I felt the first pang of anxiety. I had good reason to feel apprehensive for, as the instigator of this African-based expedition into Darkest Europe I was its titular Leader – the *obergruppenführer*. Harvey, Rex and Richard were former newspaper editors under whose lash I had worked on a big Johannesburg daily. For the purpose of this expedition they had unanimously recognised my obvious leadership abilities though they had never mentioned them during my many years as a newspaperman. They afforded me the privilege of doing all the planning of the expedition and the organising, negotiating with the cycle-hire companies and cycling outfitters, and organising the air tickets and connections. In fact, among the toasts on the eve of our departure, they had toasted me as a 'Terribly Good Leader'. I was a little embarrassed and shuffled my feet. I told them that I didn't need praise because (as everybody knew) I was a very modest person. Rex mumbled something.

'What was that?' asked Harvey.

'I was quoting Churchill,' Rex said, this time a little louder. 'I was saying that James has quite a lot to be modest about.' I was quite touched by Rex's little homily and might have coloured a little.

I had led everybody to believe that all we had to do in Passau was

3

to get on our bikes and persuade some friendly Germans to give us a little push and we'd then be able to freewheel all the way to Vienna.

'What if our brakes fail?' Harvey had asked. 'Then,' said Alan who has a way of bringing complicated matters down to basics, 'we'll go screaming through five countries and end up being pitched head-long into the Black Sea.'

I did a final check of my bike, ran a professional eye over my rear-wheel panniers, clicked my gears one final time, and re-tested the bell before announcing, with just a hint of drama that I considered befitted the occasion, 'Right, gentlemen, let's go!'

In fact they had already gone.

I caught up with them as they were balking at the formidable stream of traffic slowly crowding into the modern part of town. The city's main thoroughfare was undergoing extensive repairs and there were many confusing deviations and many temporary signs in very poor English such as *Ausfahrt, shritt fahren, radweg kreuzt* and *umgehungsstrasse*. Frankly, I find that everything in German sounds a little intimidating. To my ear even *Ich liebe zicht* sounds like an or-der for a Panzer division to move forward.

I was ushered to the front to lead the peloton through Passau. And so we merged with the jockeying traffic in much the same way that the Zulus merged with the British army at Isandlwana. The traffic immediately engulfed us and we became helplessly scat-tered throughout the city – a yellow figure here and a yellow figure there. I kept coming across my companions going in all sorts of di-rections. I had anticipated this and had suggested at the outset that if we became scattered we should find our individual ways through the town and that the survivors should muster on the north bank of the Danube where the riverside cycle track began. Obviously some of my colleagues must have been hopelessly disoriented because at one point I came across Harvey pedalling towards me and, later, as I crossed a flyover I spotted a yellow-shirted figure, head down, ped-alling furiously at right angles beneath me. Yet, half-an-hour later I came across all five of them relaxing under a tree at the appointed spot. They said they had been waiting 20 minutes.

It was not to be the last time they were to wait for me and, as always, I was greatly touched by their reliance on my leadership and their nervousness about going on without me. After a great deal of handshaking we set off. Naturally they insisted I go in front of the peloton.

[*That was after we had discovered what a 'peloton' was. 'It's a bunch of crazed cyclists trying to find their missing leader,' Rex explained in the didactic tone newspaper editors use – Ed. (Let me explain: I am not Ed. He couldn't come. I'm Harvey, and have been asked to edit this work on two dubious conditions: no fee and no deleting any hurtful remarks about me or, in his absence, Edward – Ed.)*]

Coarse cycling

We cycled leisurely in the crisp spring air along a smooth, tarred cycle track with the Linz highway on our left and the wide, swiftly-flowing Danube on our right. It was a beautiful May morning. Cotton wool clouds floated against a blue sky and our progress was under the shade of an almost unbroken canopy of giant horse chestnut trees lavishly festooned with white blossoms. [*Brisk, descriptive writing this. But let me not interrupt the flow. – Ed*] In the grass beside the track were shining yellow buttercups, white daisies, orange dandelions and the occasional patch of blood-red poppies. Sometimes we'd catch the subtle aroma of lilac blossom – the headiest of all the perfumes in the European spring.

Soon the track peeled away from the traffic and dived into a deeply wooded valley – the Bavarian Forest. We now had the river and the cheerful songs of the blackbirds and thrushes to ourselves. At one time Rex himself burst into song. It was unusual for Rex who is normally a quiet fellow. It wasn't a very tuneful song and Richard gave him a look and he settled down.

Rex, like Harvey, is a retired daily newspaper editor. Richard commented on the ecstasy of cycling through foreign lands and how both hiker and cyclists were able to enjoy the aromas and sounds of the countryside far, far more than those touring by car or bus who, literally, suffer sensory deprivation. Cycling has an advantage even over hiking – the scenery changes at a more stimulating pace yet not so fast that one does not have time to savour it. And at cruising speed one creates one's own cooling breeze. Cycling, said Harvey, is the one form of wheeled transport that cannot in any way be regarded as offensive – no pollution, no noise, little demand on road space ...

The bicycle itself is a marvellous machine when one considers how it runs on fuel such as bananas, bread and jam, beer, even duckling *bigarade*. The nice thing about this is that the cyclist has to eat it all first because the cyclist is the bike's engine and the stomach is the fuel tank.

Richard described our form of cycling as 'coarse cycling' in that it differs from riding hi-tech racing bikes just as coarse fishing differs from fly-fishing. The casual pace allows one to experience nature, even to feel part of it to the extent that one empathises with flattened squirrels and birds on the road. One's objective as a coarse cyclist is totally different from the bum-in-the air frantic pace of those on hi-tech carbon-fibre cycles that are used in road races and sometimes cost as much as a Harley.

Ernest Hemingway said cycling was the best way to learn a country's contours because you physically experience them – you sweat up the hills and there's the sheer joy of coasting down the other side.

Among my first memories as a child is that of yearning to ride a two-wheeler; of dreaming of owning one and the wonderful freedom it would offer once I had mastered the art of staying upright. I recall vividly the sheer ecstasy when, for the first time, I rode round the garden on two wheels. A bicycle is probably the first serious material thing a child earnestly pleads for in its prayers. Canadian comedian, Emo Phillips, said he used to pray every night for a bike until he realised that the Lord doesn't work that way – so he stole one and then prayed for forgiveness.

I believe the bicycle is on the edge of a golden age. They've discovered in Tokyo that cycling is faster than motoring for most trips of less than 50 minutes. Today there are about a billion bicycles in the world – most of them in China – yet the advent of the mass-produced, chain-driven cycle occurred little more than a century ago. It was an event that affected human evolution. Being cheaper to buy and cheaper to keep than a horse, the bicycle enabled more and more young men to court girls in distant communities, thus giving a wider choice of mate, resulting in a more widespread and therefore richer human gene pool.

Mechanically the bike hasn't changed much in the last 100 years of its development. Until almost the end of the 19th century its pedals were fixed to the front wheel hub which made it practically impossible to pedal up inclines. The penny-farthing with its huge front wheel and small back wheel was not only without a chain – it had no brakes. In emergencies such as when running out of control downhill, riders were advised to lift their legs over the handlebars, hold them straight out in front and aim for the softest obstacle – a bush maybe, or even a fat person – and crash into it, making sure to land feet first. It must have taken practice. Yet these front-wheel-drive bikes were used throughout Victorian times and were, in a way, the first step towards the emancipation of women. They spelt the end of neurotic Victorian modesty; the end of ankle-length dresses, corsets and petticoats. These were replaced by skirts and bloomers and all over Europe women were suddenly revealing their legs, causing men to walk into lampposts and into each other. In 1866 in Bordeaux, France, the first recorded cycle race for women was held. The girls, as they came pedalling along, bare legs working the pedals, caused such a sensation that hundreds of male onlookers collapsed the barriers along the length of the racetrack.

Cycling today is a mixture of science, sport and aesthetic pleasure. We in the *Tours de Farce* ride ordinary, relatively cheap roadsters or trek bikes with fat tyres, sit-up-and-beg handlebars, mudguards and panniers over the rear wheels to carry essentials such as map, rain cape, camera, cake fork, picture of the wife, and so on.

Darkest Europe

Perhaps I should back-pedal here and explain what led us to explore Darkest Europe. It began at the end of 2001 when in the grip of ennui I shuffled listlessly from my house to have lunch with an old friend, Lawton, who lived not far from me. While I was idly chasing a pea around my plate Lawton said something that made my fork freeze in mid-air – he told me how, a few years before, he had cycled along the Danube from Bavaria to Vienna, a distance of roughly 500km. Abandoning the pea, I pressed him for more details. He told me how he and the group he was with had pedalled along a former towpath now converted into a dedicated cycle track and how their luggage had been taken on daily to the next hotel.

'That's it!' I said. 'That's what we do! But we will cycle beyond Vienna. Next northern spring we cycle the whole way down the Danube to the Black Sea.'

'But the Danube's almost 3 000km long!' he said.

We composed a rough-scale map on the tablecloth, using peas to represent some vaguely known geographic points in Eastern Europe. After deliberation I had to agree with Lawton – we decided to cycle as far as Budapest – about 1 000km.

We needed some sort of mission – something beyond just pedalling along. Maybe an exploratory expedition to open up Central Europe and enlighten its natives to the benefits of African civilisation. Perhaps we could discover the source of the Danube for there is some controversy surrounding it, esoteric though it is. Maybe, just as my ancestors annexed chunks of Africa in the name of the Great White Queen, we could annex some land in the name of our Great Black President, or, if the locals insisted, we could trade some beads or salt for it.

Lawton, being an industrialist, tends to take himself seriously. He was to become at times quite shocked at how unseriously newspapermen take themselves. He pointed out that to discover the source of the Danube we would have to pedal *up* river. One must think laterally, I told him. We will seek it *down* river. For a start it makes for easier pedalling and the probability is that nobody has thought of looking for the source downriver before. Lawton said he was sure nobody had.

I telephoned Harvey who'd retired as editor-in-chief of *The Star* in Johannesburg ten years before and was now living on the Cape south coast at Hermanus. Harvey, a thrice-a-week golfer and already into his 70s, could be relied upon to try anything. He is a gung-ho type who had recently climbed Kilimanjaro and had competed for years in the hair-raising Roof of Africa Rally across Lesotho's 3.5km-high mountains.

'A thousand kilometres downhill,' I said. 'We'll enjoy mild exercise each day, stopping four or five times a day for a cool beer beside the river.'

'I'm in!' said Harvey. 'How about asking Rex along?'

Rex, one-time editor of the *Rand Daily Mail* – a Johannesburg daily paper the Nationalist government had often tried to close down – and of the *Sunday Express* and who ended his career as deputy editor-in-chief of *The Star* was also living in retirement in Hermanus. He thought the idea 'insane and ludicrous in the extreme' and was never to alter his opinion. He agreed to come.

Harvey said, 'Can't leave Richard out.' Harvey had forgotten something (as he often does) – that Richard was a former Natal provincial rugby captain and provincial cricket player, had maintained his fitness and would doubtless shame us all, especially cycling up hills. Mind you, so would Lawton. I phoned Richard – he was yet another former editor-in-chief of *The Star* as well as editor of the *Natal Witness* for many years – and he immediately agreed to come. I then phoned an old friend, Alan – also a rugby player and tennis player in his youth and still very fit despite a permanent injury to his spine. Alan had just retired as CEO of an international company. 'Count me in,' he said before I'd had time to explain it was all downhill.

From then on we became terribly good to our wives who, astonishingly, raised no objections to our going – at least none that would have stood up in a court of law.

I went to see Dr Peet du Toit in Pretoria who runs a company called Bike & Hike and who liaises with a European associate company, Rad und Riessen. I realised halfway through our discussion that although I'd never met Peet until then, I had written about him in a travel magazine years before. The article was about a cycle tour in Holland that he had done with his wife, small daughter and pre-school son who had ridden in a child seat. I was encouraged to see that Peet was even more overweight than I was and had been so at the time. I said to myself, 'If he can do it, so can I.' Cycling in Holland isn't heroic, of course, but sitting on a saddle for several days when you weigh 110kg is certainly heroic. Holland itself offers no challenge – one cannot really boast to one's friends or grandchildren about having cycled across a country whose highest hill comes only up to one's kneecaps.

Peet told me how quickly one gets used to long-distance cycling. His daughter, Marina, then only 12 and now a university student, had, in Holland, been scared of using her front brake which, used incautiously, can pitch one over the handlebars. And she couldn't remember in an emergency which was the back brake, the right or the left. Neither can I – even to this day. She invented her own way of stopping – she simply crashed into whatever was likely to do her the least damage. On one occasion it was a crowd at a pavement restaurant. Marina assured me she had since cycled some of the Danube and it really was very easy cycling.

Richard, Alan, Lawton and I lived within a 10km radius of each other north of Johannesburg. We arranged to meet over lunch to hammer out some sort of plan. I am not sure whether we came to any decisions at that lunch but the *eisbein* was good and we did agree on one thing – there would be no training. We practically took a blood oath on this and I communicated this to our companions in the Cape who heartily endorsed it. We felt it would be tiresome if one or two were really fit and made the rest feel inadequate. Rather we all suffer equally and toughen up as the tour progressed. They agreed that we take it easy on the tour and make four or five stops a day for a restorative beverage.

This was fine except that Lawton, we discovered, was in the habit of 'training' daily in his private gym above his palatial house in Hyde Park where he had a wondrous array of equipment including a stationary bike. A few weeks later I learned that Harvey and Rex had each bought a bike and had quietly begun a well-focused programme. Mindful of our plan to stop four or five times a day for a beer, they would cycle to a Hermanus pub a kilometre or so from their respective homes and practise drinking four or five beers. Next, I heard Richard had bought a bike and was pedalling daily up and down the steep hills near his home. Then I learned that Alan was going regularly to a gym where, like Lawton, he did rigorous 'spinning' sessions. Everybody was secretly training. Being let down by one's own team-mates is, I can tell you from bitter experience, one of the tribulations of leadership. Thus tribulated, I too bought myself a two-wheeler and immediately went into training, pedalling daily at dawn round and round the suburban stockade where I live.

Andrew McLean, a Springbok cyclist who owned a nearby cycling company, Cycle Lab, and who regularly cycled a 140km round trip to the Magaliesberg mountains before breakfast, presented each of us with a bright yellow cycling shirt made of that marvellous material that breathes as opposed to the cheaper stuff that wheezes and gasps. He gave us matching yellow-trimmed ankle socks too and Cycle Lab caps. We bought ourselves professional cycling pants with chamois leather padding to prevent sore backsides that are a common complaint among long-distance cyclists. Alan had an idea for toughening up backsides – he suggested we place a house brick on the driver's seat of our cars.

Just to hedge my bets I sought advice from another famous cyclist, Alan van Heerden, who was reigning South African veteran champion. A veteran in the cycling world is somebody over 40. (One wonders what on earth that makes us.) Alan van Heerden also owned a nearby cycle shop and he knew the classic cycle routes across Europe where he lived for some years as a professional racing cyclist. He suggested we each take a bottle of eau de Cologne to rub on our backsides at around midday to obviate pimples. Pimples, he warned, could turn into deep sores and ruin a cycle tour. He said many professional cyclists in the *Tour de France* wore sanitary pads as extra protection against saddle sores. When I told this to the team they were visibly shocked – they weren't prepared even to buy eau de Cologne let alone sanitary pads. They were even balking at wearing Cycle Lab's yellow-trimmed ankle socks.

Alan Van Heerden said, 'You'll need helmets. You must protect the brain! People have been killed falling off bicycles.' This seemed sound advice except that good-quality helmets were seriously expensive. I already had a cheap helmet and generously offered to share it – we would take turns in wearing it, thus reducing the chances of one of us suffering brain injury by 16.66666 percent. When my doctor, Mark van Niekerk, heard about the expedition he said with some alarm, 'Forget the brains and the bum – it's the heart you must worry about, especially, in your case, considering your age and your weight.' He insisted on my doing a stress test and in an anteroom I was festooned with wires and attachments like a Christmas tree waiting for the switch-on. I had to pedal hard on a stationary bicycle for a considerable time with a nurse on standby in case I dropped dead. I must have pedalled an impressive distance before, in the late afternoon, Mark remembered me. He said that, figuratively, I had probably cycled to Nairobi. He pronounced me fit. But he suggested that as it was only December and I had three months to go I should try to lose some weight.

I thought I'd try but was put off by a letter I found tucked behind my windscreen wipers in the car park. It read (seriously):

Dear Potential Client,

We speak from years of experience and our guess is that this Season of Good Cheer will leave you a lot less healthy than you want to be. But we also know that inside every chubby man and woman there is a trim, fit person struggling to get out – the former you, the INNER YOU!!!'

Because it is Christmas we offer you – for ½ (HALF) PRICE!!! – 10 (ten) sessions at our Executrim Health Club.

Just fill in the form below telling us your present state of health.

I decided I had to reply:

Dear Mr Windscreen Befouler,

Re your letter offering to release the INNER YOU within me – meaning, I hope, the INNER ME. For years I have yearned (nay, 'cried out' would not be too exaggerated an expression) to release this rather trim, handsome fellow buried very deep within me. He used to have a tan but heaven knows what's happened to it since he's been incarcerated inside me all these years.

In fact, when you come to think of it, his skin must be pretty much like raw tripe by now and maybe it's best we leave him where he is.

Your letter also asks for my present state of health but your form provides only one line composed of fourteen dots – viz: .... Upon this you seriously expect a man of my age to describe his state of health! For a man in his 20s it's OK, I suppose. He can just write 'Fine' and still have dots left over.

For over 30s it would be a challenge. For somebody over 60 it's absurd. By the time one has written just 'knees give way and joints noisy' one is off the end of the line. Yet one hasn't even begun.

If you scrutinise my coupon you will see that I, at first, wrote 'sick' before scratching it out. Then I wrote 'lousy' but you might have taken it literally. I then wanted to write 'problematical' but ran out of dots.

What on earth DO you expect people of my age to write – what with arthritis in the thumbs, tennis elbow, spastic colon and various manifestations of urban stress such as bullet wounds?

As for my mental condition, I cannot remember what I was doing yesterday and greatly fear I spent it eating. Please send me more dotted lines.

Yours truly,
Outer Me

The plughole effect

In preparation for our grand tour we had first to fly to Vienna which was to be the mid-point of our proposed cycle ride. From Vienna, after an overnight stay, we were to take a train to the starting point – Passau in Germany. We flew into Vienna at dawn on a clear spring morning and took a bus from the airport to the Wesbahnhof near the city centre where we consulted a map. We found ourselves to be in Marzahilfer Strasse and as our hotel was called the Marzahilfer Strasse Tourotel I was able to announce that our hotel must be nearby. But Marzahilfer Strasse is a long street, so the question was: which way, left or right? Here the pattern was set for the rest of our adventures. We found ourselves arguing about which way to go with each man explaining his logic and each pointing vigorously in his favoured direction. Here was the first test of my leadership. I decided to take the advice of the man who spoke the loudest. In any event he was pointing downhill and I am a downhill sort of person, particularly when dragging wheeled luggage.

We walked some distance when a little voice told me it was the wrong direction. It was not so much a little voice; it was a more of a distant voice. Lawton was shouting from some way back that they had ascertained that the hotel was in the opposite direction. It was interesting to see how, the whole time I was in the Northern Hemisphere, I would invariably choose the opposite direction to the correct one. It was to prove a severe handicap in my position as leader. I was sometimes forced to use words that should never es-

13

cape a leader's lips – such as 'Where are we?' Richard put it down to the fact that the sun in the Northern Hemisphere travels across the southern sky while I am used to the Southern Hemisphere where it passes across the northern sky. He also pointed out that water in the north goes down the plughole in the opposite direction to the south just as Northern Hemisphere cyclones go the opposite way round to those in the Southern Hemisphere. This, he said, was somehow influencing my electromagnetic biorhythms. I think he'd put his finger on the problem.

As it was lunchtime we dumped our bags at the hotel and re-grouped at a nearby 19th century pub we had spotted earlier. Here a second problem manifested itself. Some of us ordered a full beer, some half a beer and Lawton had a soft drink. We tried to work out who owed what to whom and had almost concluded matters when another round arrived and those who had a full beer first time round now wanted only half, and Lawton ordered a roll while the rest settled for a sandwich. Lawton had a habit of never eating what everybody else ate. We then spent the time feverishly writing figures on scraps of paper. Arithmetic was a subject that I failed through-out my schooling as I think most journalists do. It is why most of us are forced to take up journalism in the first place.

This weakness in the brain's left lobe has its advantages. It is the left that does the calculating and the right that perceives patterns. The right is much more fun. While the right hemisphere appreci-ates a nice pair of legs the left side counts them. Somebody who uses only the right – an artist, let's say – would be mentally unbalanced. And somebody whose left hemisphere is overdeveloped would have the personality of a herring and would prefer Rubik cubes to girls. Nobel laureate, John Nash – once described as 'the world's most promising young mathematician' – told a press conference in London in the 1990s that there was a conspicuous link between mathematical genius and madness and admitted that he went cer-tifiably mad a couple of times. I had always known that people who were brilliant at figures were bonkers. The evidence is so great one would have to be mad to deny it. I was so dyslexic when it came to maths at school that only once did I achieve an ascertainable mark. It was 7 percent. I remember at the time receiving spontaneous ap-plause from my classmates. Even Samuel Cope, our maths master,

14

congratulated me. Cope was unquestionably mad which I suspect is why he was teaching me mathematics while all his mates were having a good time chasing Germans round and round Europe.

John Nash said that for 16 years he suffered madness ranging from schizophrenia to paranoia. At one time he felt the staff at the Massachusetts Institute of Technology was 'behaving strangely' towards him. I now realise that when I attained that 7 percent mark I too was going through a brief but intense period of blinding mathematical insight coinciding with a burst of serious paranoia. I was soon over it though and reverted to zero marks. But it was strange how, from then on, brighter pupils and indeed Samuel Cope himself, seemed to be avoiding me, obviously jealous because I had shaken off my paranoia while they had not.

During this exhausting discussion in the pub about who owed what I noticed that Rex, when asked for an opinion, resorted to his usual low-resonance mumbling and I concluded he was, like me, innumerate. Little did any of us know the truth. Only much later did it emerge that he had been an accountant before he became a journalist.

But for that moment in the Viennese pub we were forced to make do with what little arithmetical insight my colleagues were willing to share. We decided to have a kitty into which each of us put 100 Eurodollars and we entrusted it to Lawton who was, after all, the only entrepreneur among us. [*In truth we were a versatile lot. For instance Alan, our other candidate for the Treasury, unknown to him and to the rest of us at the time, was soon to transform himself into a paparazzo. He was to become our official photographer. – Ed*] So Lawton was instinctively chosen as our man to handle finances. But his penchant for ordering something different from the rest of us made accounting even harder. Soon he began complaining that he must have been getting his own money mixed up with the kitty's and as a result was losing badly. Somehow, by a process I did not understand, I was then 'elected' Treasurer.

I hit on a simple method – my left pocket would be the kitty's and my right pocket would be for my personal money. This was fine but the reverse plughole effect would sometimes kick in and I would forget that the left is where my thumb is on the right. I noticed that my own supply of money was mysteriously increasing and assumed, at first, that it was simply accruing interest. Unlike Lawton, I did not whinge about it, feeling it was my problem rather than anybody else's. But after a couple of days people began noticing how rapidly the kitty was being depleted and it was suggested that the onerous responsibilities of leadership were quite enough for one man without him having to be Treasurer as well. It was at that stage we discovered Rex's accountancy past. He suddenly became the one-eyed man in the country of the blind and, just as he had feared, was unanimously proclaimed Treasurer to much applause and back-slapping. It is the office he holds to this day and even though there are times when the kitty seems to dissolve at an unbelievable rate, nobody argues in case another election swings the responsibility their way.

Women and children first

Next day we caught a mid-morning train bound for our starting point – Passau, a few hundred kilometres to the west.

The platform at Vienna's Wesbahnhof was busy so Harvey, a seasoned traveller, suggested that as soon as the train drew in he would push in front and block the door while we handed him our bags. Then we would all go for the window seats, kicking and gouging if necessary. 'I'll fight off the women and children,' said Harvey, 'you fellows see to the rest. Take no prisoners!' The manoeuvre worked like a charm and we settled in our seats highly pleased with ourselves – until a small party of what looked like German Sumo wrestlers arrived crying, '*Resvierte Platz!*' We were relegated to seats scattered all over the place – including Rex who had found a very private window seat and refused point blank to believe that the notice above it said, 'For nursing mothers only'.

We arrived in Passau at lunchtime where we had a day to kill before setting off. Having dragged our luggage from the *bahnhof* to the nearby Holiday Inn we spent the afternoon doing what one does whenever one finds oneself in an ancient city – walking until thoroughly exhausted and then stopping for a coffee or beer. We thoroughly explored the medieval section of the city and put our heads into many of the galleries and museums but because we did not read all the leaflets we had been given we missed the most famous museum of all – the Ornamental Glass Museum with its 30 000 pieces of glass dating back to before glass was invented. Rex said it was just as well we didn't find the museum because we would probably have broken something anyway.

The abiding memory of Passau was St Stephen's Cathedral, the old city's focal point. Lawton said he had seen better and was not greatly impressed by St Stephen's extravagant rococo-baroque interior with its unrestrained gilded ornamentation. As with so many baroque interiors, one comes away with the impression that the artists did not know when to stop and probably had to be ducked in the Danube to bring them to their senses. The cathedral has a battery of five madly ornate organs that share 17 463 pipes. The pipes are modern (1929) but the organs date back to the 17th century and all five can be played as one from a single console. It is the biggest church organ on earth and its huge bass pipes probably register 9 on the Richter scale. If someone were to toll the cathedral's 5-ton bell at the same time that the organist hit a low key I am sure it would cause the congregation's fillings to drop out.

[*There is already a strange omission in this tale of horror and suspense. So wrought up were we with the prospect of embarking on unknown adventures that we cared not if the cathedral bell tolled for us; whether the Richter was scaled, or whether the great 2002 flooding of the Danube had drowned many citizens on the eve of our arrival. Worse, we failed to notice in Passau a significant example of the very European culture we had come to examine. High on the West bank of the Danube stands a magnificent medieval monastery. It is linked dramatically by a great protective wall stretching from the abbey on the crest of the hill down to an ancient, awe-inspiring brewery on the river's edge. This link of religion and beer, a guide told me when I revisited the area a year or so later, exists to attract and protect pilgrims. More relevant, the brewery-link is there to comfort even foreign barbarians such as us. An excellent custom which we failed to investigate properly. – Ed*]

Chapter Two

For the first 90 minutes after leaving Passau we leisurely cruised along, keeping a tight peloton and maintaining a companionable silence, enjoying the sights and sounds. After two hours our ever-busy eyes locked on to an inn in a clearing in the forest a few hundred metres ahead. Nobody had to speak or signal or exchange glances yet, like a well-synchronised flock of finches we simultaneously wheeled to the left and, in perfect unison, swept into the drive. As we arranged ourselves at one of the rough-hewn tables under the trees a comely lass appeared and asked, '*Wasmöchten Sie trinken?*' We all recognised the word *trinken* and ordered six beers.

'*Und schnapps!*' muttered Rex. We all looked at him for a while but he said that it was well past 11 am and it *was* a trifle cold cycling under the trees, and we had, after all, just completed the first 25km of an epic ride that would, by the time we reached our destination, take us perhaps 1 000km. More importantly, somebody added, our wives weren't around with their raised eyebrows asking silly questions like, 'How can you drink schnapps so early in the morning?' Not that it was early. Quite the contrary. As Rex emphasised, it was 11 am which is very late in the morning when you come to consider it.

'After all, we are in Germany,' said Harvey, quite unnecessarily. [*Extended dialogue of this type should be avoided. Waste of time. The waitress was waiting. Anyway, by now, the time was approaching noon in South Africa. – Ed*]

'*Und schnapps,*' we all repeated.

18

The reader might wonder about our German. Indeed so did the Germans. As the leader of this expedition I realised very early on that it was incumbent upon me to bone up on the native languages of the countries through which we were to pass. I should at least be able to say 'please' and 'thank you' and announce our mission to the peasantry ...

'I am the *obergruppenführer* of this African expedition into Darkest Europe seeking the source of the Danube. We come in peace for all mankind – and womankind also, of course. We are explorers and, *en passant*, we wish to annex a little bit of your extensive lands for a colony in the name of our Great African President. Will you, kind sirs, accept these pretty coloured beads and little bag of salt for the land to the north? *Danke*, ever so.'

In the event I mastered only certain essential words such as the word for bicycle – *puffenpantenpuschenbeik*. And that for puncture – *der Bluddidammenblastenphlatt* and brakes – *überdashandellbarsschtoppenquick*.

I had also written down useful phrases from a tourist guide book such as '*Der Zug fährt sofort ab*' and '*und rechts abbiegen*' but had forgotten their meanings. [*The words could only mean, 'Our friend Zug has terrible wind – and keeps throwing up.' – Ed*]

As we planned to get to Hungary there was also the Magyar language to master. But as nobody can possibly understand Magyar, not even, I suspect, the Hungarians, I saw no sense in learning beyond one or two useful phrases such as 'Has anybody seen my socks?' and 'My aunt Edna plays the banjo'.

Thus we sipped our beer in the sunlight, discussing deep philosophical matters such as which is the more enjoyable experience – the cycling itself or enjoying a well-earned rest under the trees savouring a nation's beer? Richard, perhaps because of his legal background – before becoming an editor he was a practising attorney in London and South Africa – tends to be very measured when offering an opinion. He felt the one experience sharpened the other. He said one feels one has *earned* a beer after cycling for a couple of hours and then the continued cycling afterwards gives one the satisfying feeling that one is working it off and will soon need another. In this way one can achieve a comfortable rhythm of exercise and relaxation – never getting fitter or fatter.

Later in our journey Rex announced we were achieving 25km a litre which was generally felt to be a bit too much – too much beer that is. We tried an economy run one day and managed 32.5m/litre. [*The author forgets to mention that this called for a celebratory beer which put us back to 25km/litre. – Ed*]

On the Austrian leg of our Danube ride our average daily distance after Day One was never less than 50km although one day we cycled over 100. It was never particularly arduous unless one deviated from the demarcated route and climbed out of the river valley into the mountains. I did this occasionally but always by accident.

Best cycling in Europe

At Jochenstein we crossed the invisible German border, hardly feeling a bump, and entered Neiderosterreich (Lower Austria) leisurely pedalling through rich farmland, some of it fragrantly under the plough. The densely forested hills rose steeply from the south bank of the Danube, blocking the view of the snowy Alpine peaks that lay beyond. The Slovak border was just a few kilometres north of us.

It is said that Lower Austria is the best place in Europe for cyclists to experience the open road. Considering the length of its dedicated cycle tracks – which cannot really be classed as the open road – and the choice of places to eat good and interesting food, it is certainly one of the most pleasant places in the world for cyclists and if somebody were to say it was the best in the world I would not argue. It is just that we were later to discover in France, Italy, Ireland and England some equally delightful stretches, admittedly mostly along public roads, but just as smooth, just as peaceful and almost as free of traffic.

Much of the Danube cycle path used to be a *treppelweg* (towpath) used by great spans of massive plodding horses the size of trucks. These immensely strong one-ton *Pinzgaur*s, for centuries, towed large empty barges upstream from the boatyards, fighting against the Danube's swirling seven-knot current by walking sideways. Teams comprising dozens of horses would take a week to cover distances that even I could cycle in a day. The vessels, once laden, would be launched to drift downriver to distant centres in Hungary, Romania, Yugoslavia and Russia where, at their destinations, they would be chopped up for firewood.

Danube

TOP: Harvey Tyson (left) and the L*E*A*D*E*R at Schlögen where the Danube appeared to come to an end. ABOVE: The famous Danube Cycle Way also seemed to come to an end – in a field. I had led my companions way off track. We eventually had to carry our bikes across a ploughed field and up a steep embankment, back onto the road watched by silent villagers who had nothing better to do.

Tour de Farce 1 – Danube

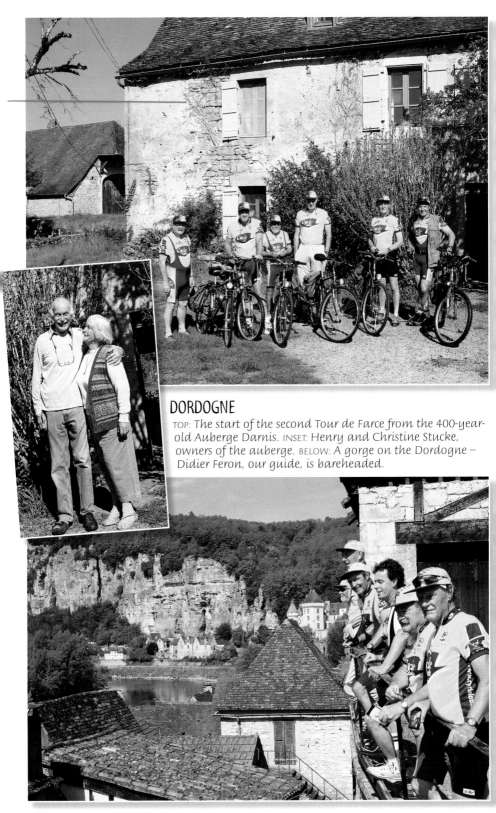

DORDOGNE

TOP: The start of the second Tour de Farce from the 400-year-old Auberge Darnis. INSET: Henry and Christine Stucke, owners of the auberge. BELOW: A gorge on the Dordogne – Didier Feron, our guide, is bareheaded.

Tour de Farce II – France: Dordogne

TOP: St-Emilion's lower square. In a cave just off this square is the stone slab on which Saint Emilion slept for years to demonstrate his love for the Virgin Mary. RIGHT: *Tour de Farce II – the full set plus Didier Feron.*

Harvey disguised as a Frenchman, Richard Steyn (centre) and the Leader (left) who is unaware of the ghostly disembodied hand of a long-dead Franciscan monk on his shoulder.
RIGHT: Rocamadour.

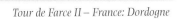

Tour de Farce II – France: Dordogne

TOP: Chateau Pichon-Longueville.
INSET: Trying to look intelligent about wine. CENTRE: The cellar at Chateau Margaux – the barrels painted with dregs.
ABOVE: Wine tasting at Chateau Margaux and the young lady we embarrassed. LEFT: Chateau Margaux.

Tour de Farce II – France: Dordogne

CANAL DU MIDI

TOP: The original team – left to right: Richard Steyn, Harvey Tyson, Lawton Christiane, Rex Gibson, Alan Calenborne and James Clarke. CENTRE LEFT: Lost. Never found out where. CENTRE RIGHT: The path along the Canal du Midi. BELOW: Two great South African editors, Richard Steyn (left) and Harvey Tyson, carbo-loading at Narbonne.

Tour de Farce II – France: Canal du Midi

TOP: Narbonne. INSET: With Richard boning up on our French. BELOW LEFT: 350-year-old plane trees along the Canal du Midi and young cyclists (comparatively speaking). BELOW: The Leader with Annie.

Tour de Farce II – France: Canal du Midi

TOP: Pie-chart fields along the Canal. CENTRE: The Canal passes high above the River Orb. BELOW: Pleasure craft emerges from the 17th-century tunnel. The canal system, linking the Atlantic with the Mediterranean, was the greatest feat of engineering since the Great Wall of China.

Tour de Farce II – France: Canal du Midi

TOP: Narbonne (I think). Look at the odd way the French pollard their plane trees.
CENTRE: We reached the end of the Canal near Sète.
BELOW: Comédie Square, Montpellier – every town should have one.

Tour de Farce II – France: Canal du Midi

After three hours of cycling we entered a narrow wooded valley where the Danube, confronted by a hard granite ridge, is forced to turn back on itself in a tight U-turn. As we approached it the illusion was that the Danube had suddenly ended against a hill. Certainly, to our surprise, the cycle track ended. As leader I was nonplussed but I did not show it. Had I consulted the map beforehand I would have realised what was happening. But only on rare occasions did any of us consult our *Rad und Reissen* map books and when we did it was mostly to see what we had missed. In retrospect we were so taken up by the sheer therapeutic joy of cycling through villages and farmlands that we were reluctant to deviate to visit *schlosses* or any of the 600 museums of Neiderosterreich – besides, these were mostly up in the hills or in the middle of cities and we weren't keen on cycling in either.

'How CAN they just end the track like this?' somebody asked. Studying the map I could see the track resumed 3km further on. But there was a cycle track on the other side. We would have to swim or pedal underwater to get to it or retrace our route until we found a bridge. On the south bank we could see a beautiful white-painted hotel with acres of neatly trimmed lawns reaching down to the water's edge where flotillas of mute swans, tufted duck, greylags and Canada geese drifted. The hotel flowerbeds looked like the Chelsea Flower Show and we could see people sitting on a long wooden sundeck drinking ale.

Rex muttered, 'Spoiled brats.'

Fortunately I was first to notice a small ferry casting off from the opposite bank and I said matter-of-factly, 'There'll be a ferry.' On cue, everybody saw it. It docked at a wooden jetty hidden from us by some reeds and the pilot invited us aboard. We told him we were looking for Schlogen. Pointing at the hotel, he said, 'This is it! You are there!'

Amazingly we'd done 47km and it was barely lunchtime.

The reader might well snort at that first day's 47km – it is, after all, about the distance that the *Tour de France* cyclists average in an hour. But *Tour de France* cyclists, their veins coursing with performance-enhancing substances, are always in a ridiculous hurry. They never stop for the occasional beer or to bury their faces in a ham roll; one never sees them leaning their bikes against a fence while

21

they admire the scenery or see them taking out a bird book to identify a bird. Neither do they have long and noisy debates over which way to go. No wonder they average over 45km/h.

Having showered and changed we joined the spoiled brats on the wooden deck and ordered German sausages and ale, noting with aesthetic appreciation the way the sun's rays turned our ale into liquid amber. We were so exhilarated after our first easy day of cycling that the thought of 75km the next day filled us with happy anticipation – in fact 75km did not seem enough as we sat there looking down the long stretch of lawn to one of the world's most spectacular river meanders.

The passage to our rooms was guarded by a huge stuffed brown bear, shot by the proprietor. Somebody thought it *was* the proprietor. That evening we dined on Vienna schnitzel in a room with the heads of many African antelope staring down at us. I couldn't help wondering at the incongruity of a springbok, wildebeest and warthog from the Kalahari ending up decorating a restaurant wall in Darkest Europe. Lawton, who has very definite views about most things, including flying saucers, bible codes and international conspiracies, expressed anger at the crassness of killing wild animals to decorate restaurants. I wholly sympathised with his view but I knew that Alan had often hunted big game. Alan defended hunting – at least for the pot – pointing out how much more humane it was to shoot an animal than to truck it to an abattoir and make it queue up to have its throat slit. We were all about to enter into noisy debate, possibly ending with some of us becoming vegans, when Richard suggested we make the subject taboo. We agreed just as we had all agreed earlier never to mention ailments. [*Agreed? All agreed, twice? This is difficult to credit. – Ed*]

Agreeing never to mention one's aches and pains was difficult. Once one gets over the age of 50 one feels a compulsion to describe one's ailments, or the merits and demerits of one's doctor to anybody who will listen. And most people over 50 are prepared to listen on a reciprocal basis. We were, medically speaking, a pretty average group of post middle-age males. Alan and Richard, being ten years younger than the rest of us, were fit enough but they were suffering from the traditional South African male complaint – skeletal injuries from rugby-playing days. Lawton, just into his 70s, had similar sports-related injuries but was astonishingly fit all the same. Harvey, the oldest man in the team, was also amazingly fit and energetic but had a couple of aggravating problems. Rex and I lacked the stamina of the others and I had clicking joints, not to mention 'the voices' in my head.

True leadership

Next day, in buoyant mood, we unhitched our bikes and galloped off in the direction of Linz. We took a quiet country road and, for a change, I was in the lead – at least for the first few kilometres for we were pedalling very sedately close to the river's edge in the cool shadow of large trees. I drew further and further into the lead and overtook a couple of farm workers – male and female – on their bikes and felt quite chuffed about overtaking even though they appeared to be in their 80s and were wearing overcoats and boots and had sacks full of something slung over their shoulders. Nevertheless, in overtaking them with slow but powerful thrusts of my pedals, I felt a certain thrill and the illusion of enormous fitness and youth.

'*Morgen!*' I said gravely. They did not respond. Probably manure in their ears.

But my excitement was such that I failed to notice that the cycle track had branched off to the left and so I continued along the quiet country road that almost immediately became a hill of Tyrolean gradient with hairpin bends. Having just overtaken the farm workers I could not now, as a matter of honour, dismount and start pushing and have them overtake me. But after a few more metres my lungs were screaming and I was forced to get off. I walked fast. I did not look back. They must not overtake me; the humiliation would be too great. The road zigzagged upwards through a thick fir forest. It became so steep that the front wheel of my bike was above my head. I contemplated walking backwards, dragging it along. My breathing became stertorous, my legs were killing me. I furtively glanced behind me. The road was empty! Ha! Even my fellow cyclists couldn't keep up with me! As the hill became steeper I recalled Lawton's words when he first mentioned his ride to Vienna – 'There are no hills to climb'. I came to a spot where I could look over the treetops and down the steep slope to the Danube itself. There, far below, was the cycle track and there, pedalling at top speed and expecting to catch me up, were my five buttercup-coloured companions. I now had to freewheel fast back down the hill, negotiate some hairpin bends, get onto the track and once more overtake the two elderly cyclists. I was in the ridiculous position of chasing after my companions who were chasing after me. I decided to stop at the first inn and reconsider my position. And that's where I found them – standing like a row of ripe pawpaws waiting for their Leader to once again take command.

I explained to them that I had cycled up the hill to see if I could see the Alps and Alan said they had assumed as much because nobody but an idiot could get lost following Europe's second-largest river. Alan often made points with which it was difficult to argue.

A short while later we had our first *grosser sturz* (big crash). We were unaware of two racing cyclists coming up fast behind us but, as they whizzed past, Richard shouted a warning to Lawton who was in front. Lawton automatically swerved left when, of course, he should have swerved right. There was a *bluddydammengrossenkrunchenkrasch.* There were sunglasses and helmets and legs mixed up with bicycle frames and as we sorted them into orderly heaps we found we had a German man and woman on our hands in a situation where it would, I suspect, have been fatal to have mentioned the war. The male was quite voluble. We explained we were from Australia where a lot of people kept left on the roads. We helped dust them down and after a rather fragile armistice they cycled on.

[*The author mentions that the German rider was 'quite voluble'. I can testify that he was more than voluble. As I was riding right beside Lawton, discussing religion or Middle-East politics, I was too preoccupied to hear – or perhaps a little deaf to Richard's shouted warning. Otherwise I too might have taken instinctive, Commonwealth-style avoiding action – swerving left instead of right. But I did hear the definitely deafening screams of 'Schyten! Furken!' or something similar as the speeding couple piled, one after the other, into Lawton's bike, fortunately missing mine. Recriminations were so clamorous and emotions so tense that I thought it would be advisable if one of the participants distanced himself from the scene. So I tactfully left before real blood (mine) was spilt. Only minutes after my colleagues had sorted out the mess and we re-*

sumed our journey, did I cycle, head down and head-on into a Mercedes-Benz. I climbed off it unhurt, with only my handlebars slightly squiff. With no way to retreat, I inspected the scratches on the Benz. The contorted expressions of the vehicle's occupants were not promising. I awaited the verbal onslaught. The driver – and his passenger – opened their doors and leapt at me. I hardly flinched, merely cowering until I realised they were shaking my hand, trying to get me to lie down, and apologising profusely in broken English.

How different it would have been back home! What a strange culture Europe possesses. Even argumentative Eddie agrees. – Ed]

We left the forest and were cycling across farmland that was very tidy. We concluded that Austrians were tidier than Germans. Even their manure heaps seemed to be squared off at the corners.

Across the river we could see the small town of Goldworth – a reminder of an unusual trade in these parts. The rivers around here are panned for gold and fished for oysters. The lime-free tributaries coming in from the northern hills bordering the Czech Republic yield the interesting combination of pearls as well as gold. Not that anybody has grown rich from this. One in several hundred river oysters contains transparent red-green 'Passau pearls' and gold is found in minute quantities.

The track ended at Ottensheim and, as we had no desire to cycle on the busy road to Linz, we took the car ferry across the river to the quieter north bank where the cycleway resumed. Here we met the couple we'd nearly demolished earlier on and they were quite gracious about it. We regaled them with stories about life in 'Sinny' and about Sinny Harbour Bridge, about man-eating duckbilled platypuses and Aussie road rules.

As we neared Linz the fields and villages gave way to factories. The cycle track merged with serious but respectful vehicular traffic. The last few kilometres took us along the left bank with Linz's industrial area, laudably unpolluted, on the other side. Soon we again crossed the Danube this time via a monumental bridge – the Nibelungenbrucke – whose wide *radweg* led us straight into the town's wide medieval *platz*. This once dull and grimy industrial city is now a clean and buzzing cultural centre rich in Renaissance, baroque and rococo architecture and whose 1 300-year-old church is Europe's oldest.

We entered Linz not as a peloton for by now my companions were obviously feeling more confident and were so far ahead I contemplated communicating with them by post. In any event I believed in occasionally giving members of the team – at least those who showed some leadership ability – the chance to assume the lead. I explained that they should take turns just in case anything happened to me such as being run over by one of the large German women who occasionally passed us, heads down and bottoms up. Or perhaps I might fall in the Danube and be swept downstream to end up in the Russian delta. They all said things like 'perish the thought' and one of them slapped his forehead saying, 'What on earth would become of us?'

By the time I entered the city my companions, brightly coloured as they were, were conspicuous at the far end of the bustling Hauptplatz, animatedly pointing in different directions each, no doubt, insisting that he alone had worked out the way to the Hotel Prielmayerhof and that going in any other direction would be an act of sheer lunacy. I was in no hurry to rejoin them for I had the map. And I had studied it. Only then did I cycle up to them.

'Follow me,' I said.

They seemed doubtful, to say the least, and darted glances at each other. I was forcibly reminded of how vulnerable these men were without a firm hand. I led them down Rudigiersstrasse, then Zartzstrasse and along the endless and busy Weissen Wolffstrasse where, to avoid the traffic, we took to the pavements as if we were Soweto taxis. As I led my companions further and further from the centre I could hear the voices of dissent growing behind me. Then *oila!* (as we linguists might say in German), there was the Hotel Prielmayerhof. My chums were gobsmacked and for one brief moment I knew how Ernest Shackleton must have felt as he led his long-marooned team from the Antarctic ice to safety.

We had a superb dinner at the hotel – all part of the package for which we had paid Peet du Toit in Pretoria. It included *kartoffelsuppeneintopl* – potato stew – which I mention only because I cannot help but admire the rococo-baroque quality of some German nouns. Then we took a bus into midtown and had a long beer under some oak trees and indulged in grading the pretty girls that passed by giving marks such as 7.2 and 9.5 – even a couple of 10s.

26

(This is another thing you cannot do with wives around.) From the main *platz*, which is the original town centre, we climbed aboard one of those childish street trains – a road vehicle made to look like a Disneyland railway train. In this we travelled around the city.

While waiting for a bus back to the hotel we spotted a meter on the bus stop that indicated the next bus would arrive in '3.5 minutes'. Harvey checked his watch and to the second the bus drew up. How do the Germans DO that?

Adolf Hitler, who was born nearby at Braunau on the River Inn, lived in Linz for some years. He had a long-term girlfriend who dumped him and is said to have broken whatever Hitler had for a heart. He never lost his interest in Linz and, bizarrely, even in April 1945 as Berlin was being systematically demolished street by street by the Russians during the final week of World War II, Hitler, besieged in his bunker, admired a scale model of how he intended modernising Linz once the Allies had capitulated. I am not sure how much, if any, of the 'new Linz' is due to Hitler's plan because our guide was either embarrassed to talk about the man or, maybe, he thought outsiders would not be interested. Instead he told us about Mozart who composed a concerto here and who loved the city.

Not terribly good leadership

As Alan had observed, it is difficult to get lost when following Europe's second-longest river (only the Volga is longer) but we managed it more than once. One night I consulted the comprehensive guidebook with its detailed maps and mentally noted that the next day, after we skirted the town of Enns, we would come across a bifurcation in the track. [*Heaven help us! 'A bifurcation' – from 17th century medieval Latin bifircatus … In our many travels, the author uttered this word only once, fortunately. All six of us were arguing over the map when it came out. We took it to be his way of venting frustration. – Ed*] The fork was, said the guide, 'easily missed'. I announced this intelligence at breakfast and it was suggested I take the lead. As we bypassed Enns the six of us maintained a tightly formed peloton. About 3km outside the town I began looking out for the 'easily missed' fork but could not remember whether it was 3km from Enns or 13. Suddenly there

27

was a distinct fork. At 20km/h a leader has to make snap decisions so I stuck out my right hand and all five followed me down a long, steep, concrete-paved hill. Immediately there were loudly expressed doubts coming from behind. I could hear Richard's voice saying, 'This can't be right!' and then Lawton called out, 'Where's he taking us?' and to me: 'Do you know where you are going?' I ignored this. I thought how quickly they had forgotten my leadership in Linz the night before. I made a mental note to talk to them at dinner about the universal code that wisely says, 'An army never criticises its generals' or, for that matter, I suppose, its *obergruppenführers.* The good thing about the track was that it was downhill, quite steeply downhill, and I was savouring leading this impressive peloton at speed, gracefully leaning our bikes into each bend.

The cries of doubt behind me increased but, as Leader, I stuck to my decision to carry on even though the track, after 2km, had deteriorated. Then it became deep gravel that became impossible to cycle on and ended abruptly – just like that – on the edge of a newly ploughed field. We had been following a ramp for tractors to haul out crops. What does a leader say at a moment like this? Rex said it for me: 'Men, you might be wondering why I brought you here this morning.'

We put our bikes on their stands and reviewed the situation. There was no way we were going to cycle back up the track with its heartbreaking incline. We were in a basin and before us was the ploughed field, the thick sods of black earth still shining from where the discs had sliced and turned them. Beyond was a high embankment along the top of which villagers had started to assemble. They were evenly spaced like thick fence posts along the skyline. They looked the sort of villagers who would point upwards excitedly every time an aircraft flew over. I could detect some sort of housing complex beyond them. They watched us standing there looking, I suppose, like a grotesque parody of a clump of daffodils. We decided to act as though we had planned the whole thing and that it was for a photo-shoot – maybe for *Men's Health* or *Lunatics' Weekly*. We took many pictures of ourselves posing in the field with our bikes, all the time bracing ourselves for the humiliation that we knew had to come. Sooner or later we were going to have to wade across the field and, in a crude replay of D-Day, fight our way up the steep bank of lank grass, matted brambles and stinging nettles and then crawl through the legs of the spectators back onto the road.

Crossing the field was like wading through treacle and it was made especially difficult because we had to carry our heavy bikes laden down with panniers. Then we had to drag the bikes up the steep embankment whose brambles clawed at us and whose nettles produced white swellings. Some of us slid back down the slope and had to start again, all the time trying to maintain an air of nonchalance. The onlookers watched in silence and without expression as we remounted our bikes and, with the dignity that befits a leader, I led the peloton into a cul de sac. When we mustered the courage to turn back the villagers were still standing there.

As the tour progressed we were pleasantly surprised to find that our backsides did not get uncomfortably sore although, on the third day, I thought I might be developing a bit of soreness despite the chamois-leather-padded pants and my gel saddle. A gel saddle is a soft sponge-like covering that pulls over the standard saddle making it as soft as a jelly on springs. For the first couple of days Harvey wore two pairs of padded pants. So did I, but in my case, as Rex pointed out, it looked as if I was wearing a full nappy.

I recalled the advice about using eau de Cologne as a disinfectant so while the others were having lunch I found my bottle and off I went to the gents to apply it. In seconds I was leaping around and, quite involuntarily, pant-hooting like a chimpanzee, shouting and dancing like a Zulu dancer who'd just been told he'd won the Lotto. Except this wasn't a dance of ecstasy; this was a song and dance of pure agony. It was as if I had sat on the lid of a Weber barbecue and it was several minutes before the fire subsided. My friends were highly amused (it takes so little to amuse small minds) and Alan then reminded me that Alan van Heerden had specifically warned us to *dilute* the eau de Cologne before applying it.

But the cycling was certainly toughening us. One morning Alan announced he was discarding his gel saddle and was not even going to wear padded pants. We solemnly saluted his courage and in a short speech I compared him with men such as Edmund Hilary and Neil Armstrong. In fact chafing and muscular aches were very minor problems. Indeed even though five of us had not cycled seriously for decades we suffered nothing more irritating than bruised ischia. [*Ischia are those two southerly-pointing, bifurcating bones of the pelvis which any sensible long-distance cyclist would have surgically removed. – Ed*]

We found the Austrians certainly live up their Teutonic reputation for efficiency and it was never more apparent than at Grein, a Swiss-looking town that squeezes itself along a narrow shelf between the Danube and the forested mountains that rise almost vertically behind it. We had ridden far that day and arrived in the town tired. We knew that it was a further 6km to our hotel – the Gasthof Zur Aumuhle. We weren't sure where the hotel was so I sought out the tourist bureau but, being a public holiday, found it closed. There were very few people about and no shops open. Behind the tourist bureau I found a tall well-groomed couple – he in a business suit and patent leather shoes, she in a two-piece pin-stripe costume – locked in a long passionate embrace. I coughed politely. They disengaged and I said, '*Guten tag*' and apologised for interrupting. I hauled out my itinerary and pointed to the name of the hotel. Displaying not an ounce of irritation the male said nothing but from his pocket withdrew a cell phone and punched a few buttons before speaking briefly in German to somebody. He then closed the phone and said in impeccable English, 'They will meet you down the bottom of the car park next to the river in 20 minutes.'

'But there are six of us with bicycles!'

'Don't worry,' he said and he then returned to the business in hand.

In 20 minutes we were aboard a bus towing a long cycle-carrying trailer. We felt guilty ending the day in a bus and wondered why it had been assumed that that was what we wanted. As the bus turned away from the river we gradually understood. The bus began labouring up a wickedly steep 5km-long, three-in-one *gruntenpuschenundpanten* mountain pass which would be hell just to walk up, let alone push a bicycle up. The driver assured us 'nobody' cycled up that pass.

Between Grein and Melk the Danube squeezes through a narrow valley and then races like a millstream past Persenberg, a major boat-building centre of the early 19th century. It seemed to me to be a perfectly ridiculous site for large boat building because of the difficulty getting them upriver where the cargoes were waiting. Lawton suggested, 'Why not haul the wood upstream by road and build barges next to loading docks?' It seemed an intelligent idea but Richard said it was not for us to tell medieval boat builders their business. In any event we felt compelled to cycle past the town for by now our ride had developed into one of relaxed scenic enjoyment rather than a knowledge-seeking exercise.

We reached Melk, a town I had visited many years before and where cobbled streets and narrow alleys are flanked by ornate ancient buildings. Melk is the founding rock on which Austria and the great Habsburg Empire were built. Melk *was* Austria once – it was called Austria for it stood as a fortress on the eastern edge of the Holy Roman Empire. It was built on a Danube cliff in defiance of the barbarians, never mind the Turks. The town is filled with such an overwhelming number of places of interest that we decided to sit under some chestnut trees in a riverside *biergarten* and, over a pint, discuss some sort of strategy. We still hadn't agreed on a strategy when the second pint arrived. Harvey said that as it was almost dinnertime most places would probably be closed so we decided to leave everything till next day.

Melk is dominated by a vast and spectacular 1 000-year-old Benedictine abbey which entirely blocks its northern aspect. The abbey's monks, for millennia, were the town's designers, treasurers, managers, brewers, vintners and educators. The abbey was an enormously wealthy corporation with God, I gather, as a sleeping partner. We decided to visit it on our way out of town next morning. In the event, we were so overwhelmed by its size and ornate beauty that we were forced to confine ourselves to gawking at just one section – a church that must be one of the world's most extravagantly ornamented. The abbey also has an incredible one-room library accommodating 100 000 volumes though the very top shelves, only reachable if one were to erect scaffolding, turned out to be merely paintings of book-filled shelves. [*There are 16 000 'special books' in that library which I visited on a later occasion – calf-bound and hand-illustrated – including one of the oldest, the Venerable Bede's work of centuries ago. Most of these books are 400 to 500 years old. We were standing in the supreme library of the Middle Ages and it was marvellously intact. – Ed]*

It was in Melk Abbey's tourist shop that Lawton lost an expensive pair of folding reading glasses in a leather case. When he realised this he let escape some words which included the Lord's name – in front of the three startled abbesses at the cash desk. We apologised on his behalf, explaining he was an Australian whom we were hoping to convert. But the Lord obviously heard all this because as we came outside we were startled by a roll of thunder and an immense black cloud. At any minute we expected to see a huge hand emerge from the cloud with a finger pointing down at Lawton, the sinner, and then, with a blinding flash of lightning, turn him crisp and brown like an *eisbein*. But to our relief the sky soon began to clear and the sun shone down on yet another glorious spring day.

We all ruefully agreed that the abbey had been worth more time and indeed we had risen at dawn to have an early breakfast in order to spend time there. Instead we had spent an inordinate amount of time milling about in the town's cobbled square. In a way it was Alan's fault for he had bought a telephone card so he could phone his wife, Joanne, in South Africa. He then offered to share it so we could all phone our wives to tell them what an arduous time we were having and how lucky they were to be safely in the comfort of their homes. This made us all feel a lot better. But having exhausted the card's bounty and having meticulously recorded how many minutes each of us had spoken, we were now faced with the task of working out who owed Alan what and this, inconclusive though it was, took up far more time than the telephone calls themselves. In the end Alan waived reimbursement. But it all left us too little time to explore Europe's finest abbey or, in fact, any of Melk's other treasures.

A couple of kilometres beyond Melk we crossed a bridge on to the left bank and after a kilometre or so we discovered Rex was no longer with us. I scanned the right bank with binoculars but there was no sign of him. We waited for a while – in vain. Harvey thought Rex might be ahead of us for he was certain that Rex knew we planned to take the left bank. In fact we were not to see him for the rest of the day. He had taken the right bank and, thinking that we were ahead of him, he was at that point pedalling flat out hoping to catch us up. Meanwhile we decided he had to be in front of us on the left bank so we also began to pedal furiously to catch *him* up.

After about 10km we spied yet another of those irresistible riverside inns. It was flying a flag in precisely the same colours as our togs – yellow and navy blue – and we felt this was an omen so we pulled in and, after posing beneath the flag to have our photographs taken, we drew lots to see who would inherit Rex's possessions should he never be seen again. I then proposed a toast to him and I said I was sure that I was expressing everybody's wishes that we'd eventually find him – not only for sentimental reasons but because he had quite a lot of money in the kitty. There was also the fact that we had a responsibility to return him more or less intact to his loved ones. Harvey confided that Pat, Rex's better half, had more or less begged Harvey on departing to look after him for he was inclined to be forgetful. I didn't tell Harvey that Arlene, Harvey's wife, had asked me to look out for Harvey because Harvey was inclined to forget things. I learned later my wife had entreated Alan similarly.

We entered the broad, gentle and fragrant valley of the Wachau – a famous wine-growing area. Apart from neat little vineyards there were ancient stone-built farms and tightly-packed hamlets scattered among the patchwork of blossoming cherry, peach, apricot and apple orchards. The valley was filled with sunshine and, in ebullient mood, we stopped at a *heuringer* where one can sample the farmer's new wine, at a price, and usually his own bread and cheeses. We lunched on bread and cheese and tried some white wines, pronouncing them 'excellent' and 'very good indeed'.

Back on the road, pedalling along in the afternoon sunshine, a young redheaded woman overtook my four surviving companions but fell into step with me and we chatted as we cycled side by side. My friends, no doubt consumed with jealousy, stayed behind in a sullen silence. I tried hard to talk to her in a normal voice, afraid she'd notice I was becoming severely stressed trying to match her pace. She had cycled well over 300km in two-and-a-half days from the Black Forest. We got to a hill and she inexorably and without saying goodbye pulled away as if motor-assisted while I had to dismount to push my bike as my gleeful friends cycled past, chirping like house sparrows.

At the end of the day we found Rex wandering around the town of Krems and for some time pretended we hadn't noticed he'd been missing. By then Harvey was missing. Harvey had raced off down the wrong road a long way back and although Lawton had tried to catch him it was hopeless. The problem was Harvey had no map and nor did he know the name of the hotel where we were staying that night. I am not sure to this day how he found the way. [*I lost my way? – Ed*]

Krems was a big, pleasant and gracious town alive with students. Our hotel – Pension Wachau – was on the edge of a large park with giant oaks in whose enormous arms students were reclining, reading.

It was two hours before an exhausted Harvey turned up. He had cycled 120km. But we marvelled at how, after a change of clothes and a beer he was ready to walk around the town.

[*Between Melk and Krems (which sound like dairy farms) the area has appallingly steep hills held together by grapevines in the middle of which is one of Europe's most intriguing centres of culture – Durnstein. We managed to miss it – like so many interesting places. I later discovered it contains universal lessons in democracy, chivalry and sheepishness – lessons of interest to all mankind except wise people on bicycles who can see at a glance what a slog it would be to get there. The best way to Durnstein, in fact, is by boat. Enter the village through its huge stone-wall defences and this is what you will learn:*]

Chivalry. *During the Crusades, King Richard the Lion Heart was not imprisoned by his devious Christian allies. The account of how a wandering minstrel came upon the English King locked in a cell in a tower is pure legend. The reality seems to be that Richard, on his way back from the Crusades, was captured by a duke in Vienna with ransom in mind. He was carried off to Durnstein in his captor's own duchy. But the law did not allow a duke to imprison a king so Richard of the lion heart was allowed to live 'free' on the duke's land, freely drinking his wine, and unpicking chastity belts at will until the ransom arrived.*
Moral: *Put not your trust in crusaders.*

Sheepishness. *There's a statue in Durnheim incorporating a lion, perhaps in honour of King Richard. The artist, it seems, had never seen a real lion so he sculpted a sheep's face to look like a lion. The result is mind-boggling.*
Moral: *What you see is what you get.*

Democracy. *Durnstein does, of course, have a tower. It belongs to the church and was designed to represent the first steps to heaven. Today it is a monument to democracy in practice. In the 1850s, the Durnstein tower was yellow, and everyone and their grandparents knew it to be that colour. But in 1986, while preparing it for re-painting, the colour blue was found underneath. Blue or yellow? What should it now be? The village was cleft down the centre on the issue. The mayor was too crafty to cast his vote either way. He would wait and see.*

Eventually a monuments commission was called in. The mayor was able to announce to all 400 citizens: 'The commission says it must be blue in the way it was designed as a passage through the sky to paradise. But you citizens can decide for yourselves – remembering that the commission will pay only for blue.'

So the tower reverted to its original blue, and no-one could be found who was ever in favour of yellow.
Moral: *When you vote, follow the money.*

Richard Coeur de Lion, by the way, continued to rampage around France grabbing treasure and 'rescuing' damsels until AD 1199 when an archer finally got him. His body was buried in Westminster Abbey, his lion-heart rests in Rouen Cathedral – and his bowels are in a casket in a church in Chalus, not far from the Dordogne. They may be the only bowels in the world that have been a tourist attraction for eight centuries.
Moral: *To be a lion heart, you need special guts. – Ed]*

I suppose if Stephen Spielberg were to make a film about it all – which well he might one day – he would call our ride into Vienna, *The Longest Day.* The six of us, as I have already mentioned, had vowed in a solemn but moving ceremony that, provided we were spared unforeseen vicissitudes such as marauding Huns, we would become the first African explorers to set eyes upon the source of the Danube. Its traditional source, in the Bavarian mountains, has been controversial because of the number of springs serving two tiny streams either of which could give rise to the Danube. Patently there would be no purpose served if we had mounted yet another expedition *upstream* and into the mountains which is why we decided to look for the source downstream especially as our one common talent was cycling downhill. With renewed vigour we set off from Krems after a breakfast whose proportions would have nauseated us had we been at home. We had about 100km of cycling ahead of us.

We decided to get there by mid-afternoon and in order to do so we would stop only if we saw a particularly attractive wayside inn. The trouble is that after a few kilometres on a hot day all inns look attractive. Come to think of it, even on a cool day. In fact, after a cold, wet day on *Tour de Farce IV* in Ireland we found every inn, even a scruffy little place with a kicked-in door and a couple of bodies outside, had an irresistible allure.

We found ourselves on the outskirts of Vienna in the late afternoon and dismounted at the first bridge to consider our position. It is a sprawling and complicated city and after scrutinising the map we discovered that the location of our hotel – the Hotel Danauzentrum – was on the far side and that between us and the hotel was a maze of roads as well as river and canal crossings. We decided to take it in stages. I was allowed to lead and I led the nervous peloton through the rush-hour traffic until a point where we realised we had no idea where we were. After that Harvey took the lead. After another half an hour and many crossings of the Danube we again lost our bearings. In the end we reverted to our usual way of navigating through cities – everybody took the lead shouting to everybody else to follow. There was no way we were going to ask anybody where the Hotel Danauzentrum was. That would be an admission that we were not only lost but hadn't got the collective IQ to read a map.

At times we pushed our bikes along pavements and then made frantic moves to weave between as many as six lanes of traffic. Rarely did anybody try to run us down. At one time we were caught on the tram tracks in the middle of a wide boulevard with peak-hour traffic on either side. It was a bit like being marooned on a narrow island in the middle of a wide African river with hippos charging down upon us and bank-to-bank crocodiles patrolling on either side. In this case it was trams, accompanied by a carillon of warning bells, thundering down upon us and I wondered which was going to be least painful – to be sliced up like breakfast ham under tram wheels or to end up ricocheting down the street from car to car like a pinball. After a considerable time we arrived among a confusion of shopping malls and a busy road junction and a little disheartened we mustered under a canopy to pull ourselves together. 'First,' said Rex, 'let's ascertain precisely where we are.' He stepped back and read aloud the name on the building under which we were standing: 'Hotel Danauzentrum'. Our hotel! After all-round congratulations and much hand-shaking and high-fiving we were shown where to put our bikes – in a dark cage in the underground car park. We were to get fresh bikes for the ride to Hungary. We said our private goodbyes to the bikes that had carried us from Germany and as I walked away I knew how Robert Louis Stevenson must have felt when he parted with his donkey, Clementine, after his travels through the Cevennes. I thought I heard Harvey sniff.

[*The author, who was understandably emotional and confused at the time, has a selective memory concerning our arrival in Vienna.*

He forgets to mention, first, that the map he produced was probably of the underground drainage system, which confused even Harry Lime. Second, the Leader forgets to mention that when Harvey – with whom I sympathise – took over the lead, the entire peloton was under the impression that we were cycling down the Danube. We weren't. We had diverted, inexplicably, onto a large canal whose waters flowed in a bifurcating direction, forcing us to enter into the milling traffic described above. No wonder we were more discombobulated than usual.

Third, the author has forgotten to mention that when we spied the name of our hotel, we set off in different directions to find the front of it. And when we finally pointed out to the Leader the great, glass-fronted entrance, he walked straight into a plate glass window and I have witnesses to prove it. – Ed]

After three blissful days in Vienna attending a Mozart concert, visiting the Schonbrunn Palace and discovering some great restaurants, Richard and Alan had to leave us – Richard to attend a conference in Slovenia and Alan a board meeting in Johannesburg. Harvey,

Rex, Lawton and I set out in tight formation for Budapest. Three days of wandering around Austria's capital had given me the confidence to tell the lads to follow me and I would show them the way across the city and on to the left bank of the Danube and eastwards or northwards (whatever) to the Hungarian border. We set off in our freshly laundered cycling clothes looking and feeling like four professional cyclists. I was surprised nobody stopped us for autographs. We found ourselves pedalling behind four elderly German cyclists – two couples – who were also on their way to Budapest. We had met them the night before and, jolly though the foursome were, we did not want to become involved with them because when one meets up with pleasant foreigners – and these German's were unquestionably pleasant – one tends to smile so much (to show what friendly people South Africans are) that one's face begins to ache. I have found that when I am thrust among foreigners for any length of time I become so nauseated by my own charm that I have to take a tablet. And there's the added strain of having to shout because foreigners understand English far better when one shouts. There was also the strain of remembering not to mention the War.

Apart from all that, the four were pedalling far too slowly for us.

We overtook them with an impressive turn of speed shouting a cheerful, '*Guten tag!*' I must then have taken a wrong turn. Fifteen minutes later, on rounding a corner, we saw them in front of us, lazily cycling along, chatting. We once more overtook them waving and smiling. Maybe they thought we'd stopped for coffee. We quickly lost sight of them. Half an hour later, panting slightly, we came round a corner and there they were 100 metres ahead cruising along still in deep conversation. We overtook them without exchanging pleasantries.

One of the problems with navigating through the city was that the cycle agents had route maps only in German and the attached translation of its contents was not terribly good. One entry, for instance, instructed us to 'ride over the bride' when we got to the river. And our bikes did not have odometers ('the Hungarians steal them,' the agents told us) so we had no idea how far we had cycled, making it difficult to know when to 'turn L at 11.7km' and when to 'turn R at 2.1km'. [*Not that we ever looked at our maps as we navigated our way out of Vienna. – Ed*]

Just outside the city we reached a stretch of cycle track that was pretty well dead straight for 20km. It was a blissful experience riding along in the warm spring sunshine on an elevated track with views of the Danube valley and its dense fluvial forest. The brochures claim the forest is inhabited by 5 000 species of animals. One can only assume the writer was counting spiders and beetles and possibly bacteria. Grassy banks fell steeply away on either side of the cycle path.

After a while we noticed Harvey was missing. Lawton went back to look for him. Harvey's chain had broken and his cycle tools did not fit his bike and the German cyclists had come to his rescue. Once more they were ahead of us.

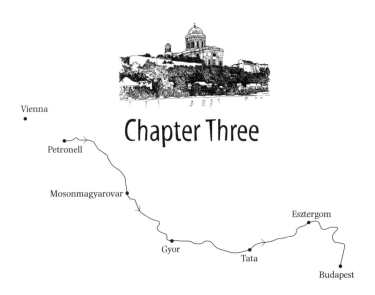

Chapter Three

Our final night in Austria was at Petronell-Carnuntum near the Slovakian border. It is a delightful Roman town whose centre is a blend of new, medieval and Roman structures dating back 2 000 years. On the outskirts we passed the ruins of its decayed coliseum and I noticed a policeman standing impassively, hands behind his back, at the side of a long hill. Only when I was about to greet him did I realise it was a dummy. In Europe they sometimes have cut-outs of policemen and even police cars because they apparently have a psychological effect on drivers. We wondered how long such things would last in Johannesburg and decided three minutes, maximum.

Early next day, Sunday, we crossed into Slovakia where the Danube passes through its capital, Bratislava. We sat under some ancient trees and had a contemplative beer. Somebody asked the waiter if he would accept a Czech instead of cash but the pun, deservedly, was left to fall to the floor and wriggle itself to death. We debated whether to 'ride over the bride' into mid-city and ordered another beer while we thought about it. The trouble is, after cycling for hours in tranquil countryside it takes a serious mental effort to ride into city traffic. In retrospect not to have gone into Bratislava was a regrettable decision for, by all accounts, it is a beautiful city.

[*The author's hindsight is accurate. We failed to cross the bride to visit Bratislava. We had forgotten that Bratislava is the olde worlde capital of one of the few nations on earth that broke away and claimed its independence without a fight – without even requiring a vote by the people involved. That's Slovakia – not yet quite recovered from the communist regime that stuffed everybody into faceless cramped apartments; stuffed the infrastructure, and finally stuffed the economy.*

However, the Philharmonic and the Opera were back in operation when we pedalled by, and the Slavic Shakespeare, Hviezdoslav, now has a statue dominating the main Slovenska Filharmonia Square. On the banks of the Danube there is another statue – a dramatic, action-movie depiction of partisans carrying their wounded to freedom. There is also a World War memorial of delightful originality – it depicts an old soldier in the trenches popping his head above a manhole cover in one of Bratislava's main streets. His life-size helmet reaches up to the hemline of women shoppers, but his gaze is too weary to see anything but the cobblestones of the liberated world. However, the most intriguing memorials are small plaques on ancient buildings, recording the loss of thousands of Slovakian children, stolen by agents of the Habsburg Empire, the Ottomans and no doubt other invaders.

Today Bratislava has laser-beam technology to light the way for tourists, and enough aching history to make them weep for weeks. It also boasts some of the prettiest girls in all Europe. We managed to bump into some. The author is about to mention them right now. – Ed]

The straight, elevated cycle path resumed but now it was busy with young people on bikes and roller-blades, some propelling themselves briskly along with ski sticks. We noticed scantily dressed young women – one wearing a crash helmet and little else – belting along on rollerblades, pushing prams fitted with three racing cycle wheels and doing at least 30km/h. Some rollerblade skaters, to reduce wind resistance, wore streamlined crash helmets and skin-tight tunics and were doubled over with their hands clasped behind their backs like Olympic ice-skaters. They overtook us at bewildering speeds. Many young women were rollerblading in bikinis and one or two were cycling in minimalistic tangas that would have fitted into a thimble. Harvey shouted over his shoulder, 'I wonder what they wear on a hot summer's day?' The mental images caused some of us to lose concentration and go off down the embankment to end up in a heap among the buttercups. One of us, quite accidentally, became entangled with a nubile cyclist, but she did not stop to hear his explanation about our Australian origins and our difficulties with remembering to keep right.

We invade Hungary

That same day we crossed into Hungary with very little inconvenience at the border – a big change from when the Russians controlled this border a few years before.

We passed through many small villages – Rusovce, Cunovo, Rajka, Dunakiliti, Dunasziget – and then our night's stop, Mosonmagyarovar. [*While in Hungary we were quite happy to split up in order to visit both Kocs and Acs, but we failed to visit romantically euphonious, easily memorised names – places such as Vamosszabadi, Orkenypuszta, Penzasas-Ujtelap, Hviezdoslavov, Almasneszmely, Radvan-nad-Dunajom, and, heaven forbid, Horny Bar just over the river.*

I remember all the places we did not go to, but very few of the places we visited. – Ed]

We were delighted with Hungarian hotels and this first one, the Panorama in Mosonmagyarovar, was a charming three-storey whitewashed structure surrounded by a riot of colourful flowerbeds. My bedroom would have delighted a girl with its prettily coloured lights in the shape of flowers and many baroque-kitsch touches to the décor. The view beyond the pink-curtained windows was an idyllic scene: a gentle bend in a stream; willow trees down one side, a small flock of lapwings in a ploughed field and a distant village. An angler stood among the reeds as motionless as a heron. It was the sort of scene from which they make jigsaws.

The hotel conservatory was bright, airy and possessed a 2.5m high standard lamp in the shape of an elaborately-dressed almost life-sized Moorish pageboy made of china upon whose head was a fez supporting a huge bowl of ceramic fruit from which sprouted a fountain of trumpet-shaped green glass lampshades which in turn was surmounted by a flamboyant spray of delicate blue glass flowers. Whoever commissioned it must surely have cried 'Enough!' just in time to stop the artist adding a pair of peacocks and a partridge in a pear tree. Whoever kept it clean deserved international recognition.

The Hungarian leg of our journey was on a B&B basis which meant we had to find our own restaurants each evening. This pleased us greatly for there are few occupations more enjoyable than browsing through an interesting foreign town looking for an appealing restaurant – especially after a physically challenging day when you feel the world owes you a good dinner. We set out on foot from the Panorama and soon spotted the Csulokjhaz Vendeglo restaurant a couple of hundred metres on. Like so many Hungarian proper nouns the tops of almost every letter sprouted an umlaut or an accent grave or a tiny circle or some other nameless symbol so that some words seemed to depict a tiny row of cottages with TV aerials.

We sat outside and ordered eisbeins – except Lawton who had chicken. We had failed to find eisbiens in Austria. Austrian restaurants claimed not to know what they were and we gained the impression Austrians considered eisbeins in the same way the English might consider hard-boiled sheep's eyeballs. But the Csulokjhaz Vendeglo knew immediately and even knew the German for them – *Schweinsstelze auf Backersfrau*. We were delighted to find that Hungarian wine (which we pronounced 'very good') was cheaper than South African wine.

The Hungarian countryside was far less formal than that through which we had come in Austria. The cows were allowed to drop their pads anywhere they liked and the villages were every bit as clean although their highly productive gardens were less orderly and had big fat vegetables and fruit interspersed with flowers such as dahlias, lupins and hollyhocks. The little inns sometimes had helpful signs in English such as 'Service to Feel Well'.

After leaving Mosonmagyarovar we found ourselves on a narrow but well-maintained cycle path between banks of brilliant red poppies and occasional hedges of elderberry in bloom. Our route frequently deviated far from the Danube, taking us across billiard-table-flat farmland. We stopped at an inn in the market town of Orth and as we sipped our beer we heard an approaching oompah band playing a rather mournful and repetitive theme. We went outside to watch as they came around the corner. Behind the sombre band filed an equally mournful line of people dressed in dark suits and the women in black. We instinctively removed our hats and composed our features. After perhaps a hundred people had passed we were surprised to see, bringing up the rear, a bride and bridegroom. A wedding party! The bride's train dragged along the tarmac gathering grit. We solemnly replaced our caps.

English-speakers in Europe are notoriously spoiled because so many foreigners speak English and good English too. What is more they are prepared to speak it even though the English themselves are pathologically unwilling or unable to speak anybody else's language. The Hungarians are no exception and as I grow older I feel guiltier about this. This guilt complex became especially acute in France the following year where, in the North, they *make* you feel guilty. Quite rightly too, I suppose. The English tend to believe that if present trends continue, most educated people in a goodly part of the world will embrace the English language. But, I have come to realise that this doesn't mean that we will all understand each other. Watching American films on television, for instance, I often have to ask my wife, 'Wotzeesay?' and helpfully she will reply, 'Doanarsmee.' I recall straining over what Neil Armstrong said during the Moon landing in 1969. He announced, 'That's one small click for a crackle and one giant grimp for mankind.' I cannot understand the Scots when they talk English. Neither can I understand Indians or black Americans – even CNN news readers when they talk about Ahdwa (capital of Canada) or Tronna (Canada's biggest city). I cannot even understand Cockneys and I *am* a Cockney. English, as it invades different corners of the world, is radically changed by the locals and I foresee it fragmenting into a plethora of dialects and eventually it will, I am sure, devolve into different languages, taking the world back to square one.

I had been to Hungary before and recalled that no word in the Magyar language shares a root with English. Study carefully the following sentence: *Ha kihult, hozzaadjuk a karikara vagott kolbaszt, a zoldborsot es az aprora vagott fott tojassal, I db nyers tojassal, sozzuk borozzuk, es az egeset jol osszekeverjuk.*

If I were to tell you that those were the words that stirred the Magyars into rising up against Ottoman rule in 1681 would you believe me? Or was this a newspaper report about a man who snatched old ladies' handbags? Neither. These words are from a cookbook on how to make a stuffed beef roll.

Obviously one can never ask the way in Hungary because it's impossible to pronounce place names:

'Excuse me, my kind sir, but how do we get to Mezokovacshaza?'

'*Ha kihult, hozzaadjuk a karikara vagott kolbaszt, a zoldborsot es az aprora vagott fott tojassal ...*'

'What? I mean, pardon? Do you speak a little English perhaps? You ARE speaking English? Ha! I mean, "Ah!" You say first we must go to Hodmezovarsarhely; then turn left for Kecskemet and then Szekesfehervar? Yes, your accent is a bit difficult to follow. You're from Torokszentmiklos? I thought so. Perhaps if I shout louder ...'

Sometimes they joke. You ask, 'In Budapest is it possible to stay somewhere between Buda and Pest? It is? *Gudzct!* But you say it's very wet? *Que?* Because it's in the middle of the Danube! Ha ha ha ha ha.'

(He will now repeat his little joke and will go on doing so until either you show no reaction or until you strike him a blow.)

The only country in the world that speaks anything similar to Magyar is Finland which is nearly 2 000km north of Hungary. This odd situation probably came about when a lost and unsuspecting Magyar from Totorkszentmiklos, asked directions to Hodmezovararhely and ended up in Helsinki's main street.

Phrase books are no good. Even if you could wrap your tongue around '*Hol van a valutabevalto iroda?*' ('Where's the bureau de change?') the reply is going to go over your head like a Harrier jet. But Hungarian names are sometimes magnificent. In fact this is true of nearly all central European names. In Austria men have STRONG names like U-boat commanders – Wolfgang, Gunter and Gerhardt. Hungarians have strange names like Gyula (which sounds like a good cheese), Karolyi (which sounds like an oriental rug) and Gombas (which sounds like a tribe in Upper Volta). The neighbouring Slavs are all named Vladimir which means 'ruler of the world'.

Mother: 'Vladimir! Sit up straight darlingski and eat your crusts, otherwise you will never rule the world!'

Vladimir: 'Yeth, Mamma.'

The neighbouring Czechs have notoriously difficult names. Somebody told me of a Czech who went for an eye test in London and the optician showed him a card with the letters C Z W I X N O S T A C Z.

'Can you read this?' the optician asked.

'Read it?' said the Czech, 'I know this man.'

But it is Hungarian names that take the *torta*. Take the male name, Gyorgyi Zsigmundczi Temesvargzinch. It means, I think, 'the mighty armour-clad warrior whose great sword can carve a path through the most congested supermarket checkout area'.

As we cycled along the flat country lanes my mind went into a state of reverie – back to 1995 and my first visit to Hungary when I watched the gorgeous gypsy dancer, Kirandulast es Uzleti (pronounced Kirandulast es Uzleti), pirouetting to wild gypsy music at a roadside café near Lake Balaton with a bottle of Szent Istvan chardonnay balanced on her head. Her dress flared out to waist height as the goulash cascaded down my shirt front. My reverie, at no extra charge, took me back to Budapest's Elizabeth Island and the Grand Ramada's elegant baroque-style dining room. The strains of Strauss's *An der schoneen, blauen Donau* were playing softly as I burrowed into the *Borjuy'ara Budapest medra*.

Kisbusszal! (Don't you love these italics? So cultured! So *szemleygepkocsiral!*)

I don't suppose I'll ever be able to afford to eat at the Ramada again. I was hosted at the time by the Hungarian tourist department and it was there that I discovered from Ramada's chef, Krisztina Korut, a great starter for a dinner party – one that I have actually made myself to the astonishment of my friends. It is called *Fustolt lazac*. The great chef himself told me how to make it. You take a slice of evenly done golden toast (let it cool); place directly upon it a thin circular slice of orange (with rind); place upon that a couple of slices of smoked salmon and put a blob of horseradish sauce on top. That's it! *Oila! Megnezhetnem!* Another dish we had was *Eroleves furjtojassa* (quail eggs in soup) but I mention this only because of the italics. (I am missing out a whole barbed-wire entanglement of symbols that go along the tops of these words.)

We left Mosonmagyarovar early and soon found ourselves at our next overnight stop, a quaint old town called Gyor. We arrived long before our baggage and had to walk around in our bright yellow cycling gear looking like a visiting team of lemons. We needed to cash some money and walked into a bank whose customers and staff stiffened perceptibly at the sight of us and a security guard said we were allowed in only one at a time.

Next day we found that our badly translated instructions on how to get out of Gyor were so ambiguous that we became even more confused than usual. Then we spotted, some distance in front of us, the four Germans – the same four we had tried in vain to overtake in Austria. At least their instructions were in their native language. Keeping some distance behind them we surreptitiously followed through heavy traffic until they were lost to sight whereupon we become lost as well. A kindly old lady cycling in from the country to shop in Gyor with a big basket on the front of her bike saw us studying a map. She stopped and, guessing our destination was Tata, did her best to explain the way. She eventually turned her bike around and indicated we should follow her back out of town, which we did for some distance but only by dint of putting our heads down and pedalling like fury. She set us panting on our way. Filled with gratitude and love for old Hungarian ladies we were soon lost again.

We eventually found the route and this is where we learned that roads that follow rivers downstream do not necessarily go downhill. For instance, when a river roars through a narrow gorge the roads take to the hills. I soon found myself on my feet pushing my bike. Lawton sailed past, hands in the air, shouting that he was not even out of top gear. If I'd found a rock of a size that could inflict a really interesting wound I would have aimed it at his head. The hills became more serious and I found myself walking long distances and sometimes, when I reached the summit, I did not realise I had done so and found myself walking downhill as well.

On the penultimate day in Hungary we hit some long and very steep hills up which most of us walked. At one point I saw Lawton pedalling up a vertical climb through a haze of red bishop birds which turned out to be my own red blood corpuscles swirling around in my vitreous humour.

I will confess that when we reached Sventendre which is an ancient and attractive town set high above the river we decided to rest there and catch a mid-afternoon boat into Budapest because we knew the ride through the city to our central hotel was likely to be fraught. I'd been to Sventendre before and rather liked the place with its interesting antique shops even though it is dedicated to trapping tourists. We eventually wheeled our bikes on to a smart ferry and thoroughly enjoyed the cruise and the gradual unfolding of the beautiful and elaborate Hungarian capital with its breathtaking architecture. The Gothic Parliamentary Building on the Pest side of the river is probably the most beautiful government building in Europe.

When I was last in this city it had just emerged from half a century under the Russians who helped establish the People's Democratic Republic having undemocratically shot anybody who didn't like their interpretation of 'democratic'. The greyness of communism was, on that first visit in 1993, still apparent in the featureless rows of identical concrete apartments designed and built by engineers. There were still some of those primitive plastic cars around – the Trabants. The 60 000 Russian garrison had just left the city and in the flea markets one could buy Russian officer uniforms, and piles of Russian medals, coins, notes and flags. I bought four babushkas and the stall-holder was so delighted he pinned a medal to my jacket – I became a Hero of the Soviet Union.

We were surprised to find the four Germans on the ferry and they said they were staying at the same hotel. I won't say we all began tugging at their sleeves begging for them to lead us across Budapest but we did make some sort of arrangement like that. In the event we did indeed follow them and we were a little comforted when it became apparent they were lost. But we happily followed them, sometimes doubling back along the same old boulevards that were, in effect, architectural exhibitions – Romanesque, Gothic, Renaissance, Byzantine and neo-everything. Some buildings, including our hotel, bore the scars of the German occupation and the assault a decade later by 6 000 Russian tanks when the populace rose up against the Soviet occupation. Today the greyness has almost disappeared and we voted the city every bit as elegant as Vienna. It is now prosperous and friendly and because of its quaint and wonderfully efficient underground train system whose neat, clean little stations with their glazed tiled walls look like 19th century public bathhouses, it is easy to get around. Budapest is a much underestimated capital.

Appropriately, some might think, we spent our final afternoon at the Dreyer Brewery in Budapest – Hungary's largest brewery whose chief executive was a friend of Alan's. The brewery is one of many across the world owned by South African Breweries. What interested me was that when SAB took it over after the Russian occupation it was employing 5 000 and making a loss. Today it produces far more beer and is highly profitable, employing only 900. To compensate for the job losses its new and growing prosperity has triggered all sorts of new enterprises and outlets and, therefore, job opportunities throughout the country.

Our final dinner was at a splendid restaurant called Fatal.

Chapter Four

I have had a fascination for France ever since I was at school in England. I recall listening to the six o'clock news during World War II and hearing, after Alvar Lidell had read the bulletin, the did-did-did-daar ('V for victory') Morse code signal and the solemn voice intoning, 'This is London ...' Then would follow the cryptic messages from Britain's espionage chiefs to the French Resistance across the Channel. We all knew that these brave partisans faced unspeakable horrors if captured in Nazi-occupied France. As a ten-year-old I watched, day after day, thousands of marching troops passing our house in the Warwickshire countryside as well as endless convoys of tanks and lorries all draining south to the Channel ready to cross to Normandy to liberate France.

My elder sister was learning French but my teachers decided I was too dumb to do that and, instead, I had to take up woodwork classes for which I had neither the enthusiasm nor the aptitude. Everything I made was what one would call 'collapsible'. Just before my final year it was decided I would probably do better at French after all, but by then it was too late and I learned little beyond 'the pen of my aunt is in the field', a phrase for which I never found much use.

My first contact with the French had been as a schoolboy when I joined the 1st Streetly Boy Scouts on the Staffordshire/Warwickshire border. After the war, for a reason nobody ever fathomed, my patrol was invited to take part in one of the first post-war international 'jamborettes' on Cannock Chase (*The Yellow Six* – Penguin, Johannesburg and Brewin Books, Birmingham). We were allocated a small roped-off area on a grassy slope within which we had to pitch our tent, light our campfire and erect a flagpole. Because of the way the alphabet goes our site was next to the French site and it overlooked a deep, dark woodland that filled us with fear. Many things filled us with fear, but particularly dark places because, during the war, as far as we were concerned, the dark was full of spies hoping to overhear some careless talk about the movement of His Majesty's battleships or the whereabouts of the Eighth Army.

 Our tent, being an ex-British Army job bought for a song at the Army and Navy Surplus Store, was extraordinarily large and heavy. The man told us it had belonged to Field-Marshall Bernard Montgomery and that it was bulletproof. Erecting it took hours and great co-ordination and much shouting and sometimes squabbling and shoving each other around. Halfway through erecting it the French contingent, having long ago completed their astonishingly neat camp, and themselves looking insufferably antiseptic, came to watch us. We had been told to be extra nice to the French because they were still a bit shell-shocked, and because of *Entente Cordiale* (which we thought must be a special French fruit drink and, if we were nice, they would share some with us).

 Frustrated though we were, we shouted jolly things to them in dreadful French but, halfway through getting our tent up, one of the French sniggered and our bonhomie snapped like a perished guy rope. Laidlaw, who knew some German, shouted at them in that language but with such an exaggerated guttural accent, and with so much goose-stepping, that it brought World War II flooding back in vivid Technicolor and Stereophonic Sound. The French fell back. As they did so, 'the Welsh Kid' (as we called him), whom we had let join us to demonstrate our level of cultural tolerance, shouted after them in Welsh for quite a long time. He might have been a small kid but he had a very large mouth and, for some distance around all dropped what they were doing to listen, enraptured because, although they could sense the richness of the language, they had no clue what language it was. Nobody had. Nobody, that is, except the camp commanding officer, District Commissioner Lieutenant Colonel Sir Llewellyn Llywarch-Griffiths of Aberystwyth.

51

I was at the time on my stomach retrieving some jam that we had spilled and I became aware of a shiny brown shoe a few inches from my face. Next to it was a second and matching brown shoe. From each shoe arose a very straight sock topped by a knobbly knee. As I raised my eyes I could see a pair of well-ironed military shorts and a shirt bearing so many medal ribbons it looked like a stamp collection. Above the shirt was the splendid moustachioed head of the colonel. Sir Llewellyn, visibly shaken by the tirade, reminded us that the Scout Law said 'A Scout is clean in thought, word and deed'. Everybody looked at the Welsh Kid. The chief lambasted us for some minutes and then, with unnecessary emphasis, carefully wiped his feet before stepping over the rope into the French Scouts' space. We lost many points because of this episode, but we watched in fascination the skills of the French.

It was Scout Law that when making a camp fire one had to dig up a table-sized piece of turf, roll it up neatly like a Swiss roll, and store it. What amazed us was that the French actually managed to do this. The idea was that when the camp was struck, we would rake the campfire ashes flat and replace the grass. Hey Bisto! Not a trace of Man. But in our case there were many nauseating traces of Boy. Apart from a large area of fire-blackened grass at our site there was porridge everywhere – porridge that never seemed to biodegrade. Neither, we noticed, did it attract ants or other creatures. In fact it killed grasshoppers. It was the same with our stews. One night we offered some stew to the French as a token of appeasement but they drove us off with sticks.

Nevertheless my interest in the French was unabated and when I was 16, on the very afternoon of my last day at school, having learned all there was to know about just about everything (except French and woodwork – oh yes, and mathematics) I set off on foot for France. I was laden with all sorts of quite advanced military equipment bought for next to nothing from the Army and Navy Surplus stores. You could buy a frigate in those early post-war days far easier than you could buy liquorice all-sorts. For a start frigates weren't rationed; sweets were.

When I landed at Calais festooned with army billycans, a huge knife, and an army pup tent, I am sure the French thought the British Expeditionary Force had returned. I walked through Paris, sleeping on street benches and, after a month or so, reached the Mediterranean, living mostly off beef cubes and flour and food stolen from fields and orchards. I met with a lot of kindness from the French. You could travel alone in those days without getting murdered too often.

I became something of a Francophile but my later visits to France were nearly always whistle-stop tours as a journalist. I was delighted when, in 2003, my five cycling companions showed not only enthusiasm for a second *Tour de Farce* but were unanimous that it should be in France. They also agreed it would be in May. [*It just goes to show how easy it was to go gathering nuts in May. – Ed*] They also agreed that I should once again be their leader and bestowed upon me the privilege of liaising over dates, making the arrangements regarding travel, airfares, accommodation, bicycle hire and kit. Richard told me, 'It is our small way of demonstrating our confidence in your leadership.'

Alan, Lawton and I took three French lessons in order to exchange pleasantries in French so that the locals wouldn't throw rocks at us. I wrote pages of notes and became, in my own estimation, if not the teacher's, quite advanced. I learned to say, '*Quelle jolie vue!*' which, I was assured, is what to say if one crashes into a peloton of angry French bicyclists. I was confident that my knowledge of French would greatly enhance my value as leader.

I went to see Pierre Saliba who is in the Foreign Legion of the French tourist industry stationed in South Africa. Pierre, once a serious cyclist himself, headed the Johannesburg office of Maison de la France. After some discussion Pierre suggested we begin by cycling down the Dordogne River to Bordeaux and the Atlantic. But we also wanted to reach the Mediterranean. He then suggested that we then double back from Bordeaux and cycle south-east via Toulouse to the Mediterranean following a four-centuries-old canal system that links the two seas. *Merveilleux!* Canals, after all, cannot possibly flow uphill. There were difficulties though, the foremost being hiring a set of bikes for the entire distance. Booking accommodation at appropriate distances also proved a challenge.

Once again we would be following the inevitable downward flow of a major river, the Dordogne – a point that was well received by my companions. But had I consulted the map more closely I would have seen that the route in fact does not follow the river at all; it criss-crosses it, zigzagging up and down hills – a roller coaster of a route. The Dordogne, unlike the Danube with its vast flat floodplains, cuts deep into the soft, chalky landscape and only along parts of it is there room for a road alongside. [*I told him so, I told him so. If it was flat along the Dordogne, how come there were so many castles built on hilltops? How come this place formed the Defence Line between French troops and English invaders in medieval times? Remember our oath, I told him – remember all our oaths on those gruelling Hungarian hills – and our promise never again to cycle in sight of hills. – Ed*] Our route comprised long downward slopes and equally long upward ones. We later worked out that five minutes of fast downhill can indicate one hour of uphill to follow. An optimist would put it the other way round: an hour-long climb is usually rewarded by a blissful five-minute descent.

Once we reached Bordeaux we intended to turn back on our tracks and travel south-east to follow the Garonne River for a while. The Garonne is navigable for only a short distance from the Atlantic and then the Canal Lateral à la Garonne links it to the more famous Canal du Midi at Toulouse from where the canal's course leads to the Mediterranean port of Sète. The canal system was designed in 1666 so that cargo vessels coming from the Atlantic and destined for southern France could avoid having to go all the way around the Iberian Peninsula. Because of the limited time at our disposal the French advised us to miss the Garonne altogether and, instead, take a train from Bordeaux to Toulouse where we would pick up the beginning of the Canal du Midi and cycle along its length to the Mediterranean.

Determined to be as fit as possible for *Tour de Farce II*, I went into serious training. I was then living in a cluster development in a suburb called Lone Hill, on the northern extremity of Johannesburg. It was a typical South African suburban stockade with a security gate and surrounded by high walls topped with razor wire and electrified wire hiding, in this case, Dutch colonial-style houses. At the crack of every dawn I would leave the stockade and set out to walk a 3.7km circuit around Lone Hill itself, doing it in 40 minutes. But for the speed bumps I could have walked it in far less time. One morning I had a strange experience. There was at the time an ostrich farm in

Lone Hill and as I passed it I heard, for the first time in my life, the boom of a male ostrich. It sounded like Paul Robeson, the celebrated Negro bass singer of *Old Man River* fame, throwing up a bucketful of oysters – 'orpp, orrpp, OOOORRP!'

Sometimes I'd do the circuit twice and I became a familiar figure leaning panting against trees. By February I was able to treble my speed – by riding a bicycle. On the day before we left for France I trebled it again by going round in my car. There is a great deal of mental therapy in walking or cycling round one's neighbourhood while the first sparrows are still clearing their throats. I enjoyed it immensely and I would leap from my bed with my usual cry of 'Torah! Torah! Torah!', jump into my tracksuit, do a quick press-up and go. Others on the road would greet me a trifle nervously because they knew that anybody over the age of 40 at large in the half-light of dawn was probably dangerous.

On one occasion, halfway down the first hill but still on the main road, I found I had put my tracksuit trousers on inside out and back to front and that the flapping that had been worrying me was the white lining of my pockets flapping like goose wings from my hips. I tried to tuck them in but they would immediately flop out again. Because the trousers were back to front as well as inside out it was impossible to put my hands in my pockets and thus stop the flapping. I thought of going home to change them around but I was by now a kilometre down the hill from the house. Then the voices in my head began. They said, 'It's still not all that light – change them now! Quick, while there's nobody around.' (I often hear these little voices and if ever I find out from whence they come I shall set upon them.) What if a neighbour drove past on the way to the village's 24-hour gym? How would I be able to explain myself standing there, trouserless, at dawn?

'Go for it!' said the voices.

There were no houses around – just the village shops on one side, all shut, and the brooding fire station on the other. I had my pants halfway down when I heard a sudden noise to my left and was then blinded by a powerful searchlight and the deafening roar of a bull-horn – a fire engine was about to emerge from the station! I like to tell myself that in pulling up my pants my movements must have been so subliminal that they would have deceived even the world's fastest

55

lens let alone the bleary early-morning eyes of firemen. That's what I keep telling myself. It grew light and I continued to walk briskly with my conspicuous flapping wings, greeting each jogger, cyclist and pedestrian with a grave nod.

When, in my newspaper column, I gave a rough outline of our plan to zig down the Dordogne and then zag down the Canal du Midi it resulted in an e-mail from Henry and Christine Stucke in the *département* of Lot in the Upper Dordogne valley. Christine and Henry own a huge 400-year-old stone auberge – formerly a farmhouse – in the tiny hamlet of Darnis near the village of Gramat. The Stuckes felt the auberge would be good place for us to acclimatise before our run down the Dordogne River to Bordeaux and Christine invited us to be their guests for two days. The Stuckes spend the northern summer in Darnis and, incredibly, the southern summer in South Africa, living in a rambling farmhouse 1 500 metres from where I now live. Henry is a retired Anglo American Corporation mining engineer who looked after mines in Asia, America and Australasia. He bought the derelict French farmhouse in 1975.

He advised us that on arrival at Paris' Charles de Gaulle Airport we should take a train to Gare d'Austerlitz in central Paris and from there a train to Brive-la-Gaillard (one doesn't pronounce the 'd'); then catch a smaller train to Rocamadour; then an even smaller train to Bretenoux (don't pronounce the x) and then a train so small you can hardly see it to a village where you don't pronounce any of the consonants at all. In the event the journey was made much simpler by Christine picking us up from Bretenoux and so we arrived in style at the Stuckes' enormous, three-storey homestead with its comfortable old furniture.

When Henry bought the farmhouse the hamlet of Darnis boasted a cluster of little stone houses, a communal 17th century stone-built baking house and even a small school. Today only one other house, a barn, a water trough and the ruins of the baking house remain – a manifestation of the post-war depopulation of rural France. All around are low stone walls, soft rolling countryside and the occasional oak grove where local farmers use dogs to seek out truffles which are as valuable as gold nuggets these days. They use dogs because if they set out with the traditional sniffer pigs unscrupulous neighbours would leopard-crawl after them to find out where the truffles are. A man and his dog attract less curiosity.

Despite the rather paradisiacal aspect of the Dordogne Valley, especially the upper Dordogne, the region has been the frequent scene of hellish religious wars. It was in this valley that, in the 14th century, the French and the English got together, so to speak, during the Hundred Years' War. As a consequence almost every town around this region is a former citadel on a steep hill. [*Didn't I tell you so? –Ed*] This is mainly because of the English who, for 400 years, occupied this region and often behaved like defeated Liverpool soccer fans – hence, I suppose, the term, *Pommes de terre*. The One Hundred Years' War ended with the French wining by 22 – 10, if you count the battles. The event seems to have included a lengthy period of injury time because the war, in fact, lasted 116 years.

The Stuckes, bit by bit, restored and converted the farmhouse by offering free accommodation and meals during off-peak periods to anybody who was willing to stay a minimum of two weeks and was prepared to work a 35-hour week, flexitime, helping with the restoration under Henry's supervision. A couple of teachers came along one year and under Henry's direction built a uniquely styled spiral staircase of heavy timber and steel – this despite never having wielded even so much as a hammer in their lives. Just before we arrived a young woman arts student from Cambridge had, much to her own surprise, neatly oak-panelled the bedroom in which I slept. I felt it incumbent upon me to offer the Stuckes the services of my five companions suggesting that, under my supervision, they could carry stones up from the quarry to repair the old bake house, but the offer was declined.

We spent two days with the Stuckes who set about fattening us up for our epic journey. We ate hearty farmhouse breakfasts and gourmet dinners – dinners that we declared, with absolute sincerity, to be among the most memorable in our collective 414 years' experience of enthusiastic dining. I noticed that when Henry had almost finished his soup – made from courgettes and leeks and typical of the region – he poured a little red wine into his plate, swilled it around and drank it. It was, he told us, a quirky Quercy peasant custom known as *cabrol*. The main course was a famous French recipe known as *magret de canard*. I doubt we'll ever experience the like of it again.

Next day, to ameliorate our alimentary excesses, we walked 12km along the winding Alzou River gorge in the footsteps of the penitent medieval pilgrims to Rocamadour, a near-vertical village rising in stages against a towering grey limestone cliff. Some of its buildings are partly carved from the cliff itself and the whole is surmounted by a 14th century chateau. Our consciences, still racked by the deadly sin of gluttony, compelled us to climb the 200 steps to where the pilgrims worshipped and then even further up to the very top where Henry and Christine were waiting to drive us home. But some of us, feeling we should pay further penance, and worried that dinner that night would be as memorable as the previous night's, elected to walk every step of the way back to Darnis. This time we took to the country lanes through sheep farms and lavender fields. Back at Darnis, our sins absolved, we fell upon yet another duck dish – *confit de canard* – with an enthusiasm that would have badly frightened any auberge keeper except the Stuckes. I had become a canard junkie.

Pierre Saliba had warned us that the 3 000km-long *Tour de France* would pass along our route. Harvey said that as all six of us were wearing yellow jerseys, a colour that only the leading man in the *Tour de France* is allowed to wear, we might cause confusion. Disappointingly the Tour de France was scheduled for a time when we would already be back in the bosoms of our families, trying to get them to listen to our own stories of superhuman endurance and derring-do.

Performance-enhancing substances

'Providing we all remember to cycle on the right-hand side of the road,' I said, giving Lawton a meaningful look, 'we need have no fears.' The team did have fears though. Richard admitted he was worried about the route I had chosen. This was tantamount to questioning my leadership. Was it not I (or me, perhaps) who, only the year before, led them nearly 1 000km along the Danube Valley, hardly ever getting lost? Lawton subtly hinted that it was a trifle difficult following a leader who lagged so far behind the peloton: 'How the hell can we follow somebody who's behind us all the bloody time?' I reminded him that Napoleon rarely rode in front of the *Grande Armée*; nor did Montgomery bowl along in front of the Eighth Army; nor did Lord Cardigan ride in front during the Charge of the Light Brigade, clever fellow. Rex concurred, saying he doubted any of them even had a bicycle.

At dawn on the third day at Darnis a bus carrying a rack of cycles arrived. Didier Feron, the young and good-natured cyclist and guide who drove the bus said he'd been told by Maison de la France that we were elderly journalists who needed to be bussed to each town where we would pedal around tasting wine. We were standing outside the Stuckes' great stone house and we drew ourselves up to our collective height (10.4 metres) and said we intended cycling the entire distance west to Bordeaux and east to the Mediterranean. Harvey inadvertently spoiled the moment by clapping a hand to his ear and mumbling: 'Hey fellers, wait! Where's my hearing aid?' Didier regarded us with a measured gaze: his eyes slowly travelled from man to man and then from our cute little yellow cycling socks to our bright yellow and blue cycling clothes to our caps emblazoned with 'South Africa'. [*The caps were Richard's idea. We had each bought one at Johannesburg Airport not, as Richard explained, to proclaim our nationality but to ensure we were not mistaken in France for Americans or British who were, at that time, very unpopular because of the Iraqi invasion. – Ed*]

Didier explained he had been instructed to take us in the bus to Sarlat where at 11 am we were to meet *monsieur le maire* and, after lunch, to meet the regional head of tourism. I told him we had made it clear, verbally and in writing, that the object of the exercise was to cycle every inch and, indeed, every millimetre, of the route. We would arrange our own interviews. Didier then phoned Johannesburg and after a few words announced with genuine enthusiasm that he would cycle with us. This was very generous of him because it meant that at the end of each day he had to hitch a ride back to our starting point to collect his bus and bike trailer.

Henry improvised a starting flag out of a tea towel and, when he ceremoniously dropped it from a raised position, we set off on the first leg of our ride across France following the Dordogne Valley.

[Readers will have noted with alarm that so much preparation – including training, planning, and pre-travelling – is required in an expedition of this nature that a whole chapter is required to de-

scribe it. Rest assured that the author's ramblings on the subject will be ruthlessly edited from now on.

However, in the constant, though forlorn, search for the whole truth in this work, it is necessary to record that there have been many pitiful and occasionally painful lapses in preparation for Tour de Farce *expeditions. The author has failed to mention one that occurred at this very point in the saga – a lapse that threatened to bring shame upon the entire project. The case was this: When one assumes the well-worn role of travel writer, hosted in foreign climes, one also has to assume certain labels, duties and responsibilities. At least one has to be seen to wield pen or camera. Most of the Tour de Farce team had been doing the former for longer than anyone could remember. But Alan, who had been a business executive most of his life, now had to become our official cameraman. The time allowed for his training and preparation was pitiful. As we posed for the team photo at the start of* Tour de Farce II *– with hosts, with officialdom, with bikes and with fixed grimaces – Alan looked up from his camera and with genuine perplexity asked: 'When my lens is on f/11, does it make things bigger or smaller?'*

'He's kidding! He's kidding!' the team cried in unison. But it was a close call.

Let me not further interrupt your reading, for this is no time to pause. You still have to learn how our lost Leader solved the dilemma of where we were due to stay on our first night along the Canal du Midi. – Ed]

Henry's tea-towel starting flag fell at Darnis. *Tour de Farce II* across south-west France was on. I tried hard not to pant as we immediately hit a long uphill slope from Darnis and was surprised to find that after five minutes I was way out in front. Then I heard distant shouts from my five companions – I had turned right instead of left. The dreaded plughole syndrome had struck again. I admit to a poor sense of direction but I am no more ashamed of it than a man who lisps is ashamed of the way he speaks. James Cook was the same. Look how he dithered when he got into Turnabout Sound in Alaska. Look how Columbus tried to get to India but ended up in the West Indies. Nevertheless it is difficult behaving like a leader when you have to cycle back to where your team-mates are standing rolling their collective 10 eyes and drumming their collective 50 fingers on their handlebars.

The countryside was at its best and the verges aflame with bright red poppies. The grass in the meadows was high as a Charolais' eye and the morning was set to become another warm spring day. Rex, once again, broke into song that was mercifully replaced by wheezing as we climbed a steep hill. On cresting the hill we were confronted by the longest downhill in our experience. As we passed a cluster of dwellings – the hamlet of Pouch – we heard the cry, '*Vrystaat!*' – that quaint South African expression which literally translates to 'Free State!' but which is equivalent to the Frenchman's '*Vive la France!*' or the Briton's 'Up Chelsea!' By now we were descending at near-terminal velocity. We caught a glimpse of the person who shouted and he was waving a South African flag. We learned later it was South African potter, Gavin Bell, now living in France and whom we'd met at the Stuckes'. We hadn't the courage to jam on brakes and we knew that if we stopped it would mean a long haul back up the hill to greet him, so we waved and plummeted on, gobbling up the first 10 of the 60km we had to do. We experienced severe G forces as we pulled out of our dive and crossed the Dordogne.

The Dordogne is a spectacular river that in parts cuts deep gorges between sculpted limestone cliffs. Ahead of us we could see the start of a long climb just beyond St Sosy village. We also spotted a café next to the river. We found a table where we toasted in coffee the climb that loomed ahead of us.

This is one of the most attractive stretches of the Dordogne. We were told though that the Upper Dordogne to the east of Darnis was even more dramatic and beautiful. We were in limestone country and that meant caves and these included the famous Grotte Lascaux discovered in 1940 by boys following their dog down a hole in the hillside. The caves shelter boldly coloured giant murals – possibly 35 000 years old – depicting the extinct auroch, grandfather of modern cattle, as well as the extinct European bison and other animals. The murals would be hailed as being brilliantly executed even if done today. Alas, the caves were too far for us to reach by cycle. Somebody said that this valley is also where 30 000-year-old Cro-Magnon man lived and this made us all feel a little younger.

The valley is rich in castles, vineyards, farms and villages in which even the most unprepossessing cafés offer gourmet meals at modest prices and invite travellers to sample wine, cheese or pâté. The valley is one long smorgasbord.

Sarlat itself is one of the most meticulously preserved 9th century towns in Europe and has a fascinating open-air market where fish and fowl, red meat and cheeses are presented in a way that only the French seem to be able to achieve. Every item of vegetable and fruit appeared to have been polished – even the lumps of truffles (which resemble dog faeces) are as elegantly presented as one could wish with dog faeces. The Hotel de Selves where we stabled our cycles and slept that night was very near the centre and as we walked from it, slightly bow-legged, into the heart of town that evening we felt like six baddies in a cowboy film. ('*Écrevisses!* Hide zee daughters! Zee *Six Formidables* have hit zee *ville!*') We were searching for an attractive outside restaurant, preferably, said Rex, one that killed snails humanely. We found it in a cobbled square. There were no visible telephone lines or TV aerials because by-laws insist that all have to be hidden so that the medieval skyline remains unadulterated.

I was about to address my third roast duck in three days when Richard, without a word, rose, walked into a nearby shop and came out with a ridiculous loaf-sized white porcelain duck whose neck dangled below its body and was festooned with a blue denim ribbon. 'Elizabeth will like this,' he said a trifle self-consciously. Then Harvey rose as if hypnotised and without a word he too returned with a similar duck. These crock ducks are meant to be placed on the edge of shelves so that their heads can hang over the edge. 'For Arlene,' he said. We all nodded. Then I found myself getting up ... Next day, faced with having to transport fragile ceramic ducks for the next two weeks across France, we wondered what made us buy them. It was either some kind of hypnosis or it was conscience. Conscience? Perhaps it's because men aren't supposed to enjoy themselves away from their wives and when one gets home they ask (after you've dispensed your ducks and other conscience gifts usually bought hastily and expensively at the airport), 'Did you miss me?' There are several possible answers but only one safe one and that is, 'Of course! I thought of you all the time – in fact I couldn't wait to get home.'

Avoid such answers as:

1. How do you mean?

2. It depends what you mean by 'miss'.
3. Sometimes.
4. Are you kidding! With all the parties and frolicking?

[*It needs to be recorded that the duck decoy didn't work. In my home the ceramic duck that I had carried clear across France was banned from our living quarters and banished to my upstairs study where it still perches on the top bookshelf, head hanging down as it surveys me reproachfully. In my colleagues' homes their spouses thought it was kitsch. I happen to know that in the end the author gave his to his granddaughter, Natalie. – Ed*]

It soon became obvious to us that the Dordogne Valley was worth a week to ten days but there was nothing we could do except enjoy, like typical travel writers, a brief sample. The valley presents a vast choice of attractive capillary roads and interesting sites but we had to accept that we were merely reviewing the cycling opportunities and often had to take short cuts along busy highways which we would normally have avoided. [*Capillary roads are filled with bifurcations unfortunately; not to mention inclines, sharp bends, oncoming tractors, puddles and sheep. They don't have direction signposts, even in Italy or Ireland, we were later to discover. – Ed*]

One memorable day we spent cycling from one delightful wine-producing village to the next. We came to a long hill and I was reduced to walking beside my bike. In fact my bike had been struggling beneath my weight and it needed a break and in any event walking enabled me to more fully savour the view down the Dordogne Valley. Halfway up we came across a quaint and irresistible inn perched on an escarpment and we stopped for coffee on the patio. Despite the brilliant sunshine there was a chill breeze and Rex suggested we should have a cognac with our coffee.

'Cognac! It's only 10 am,' I exclaimed with a sense of *déjà vu*.

Everybody looked at me as if I had just said something.

'After all, this is France,' Harvey said.

'A cognac! Yes! *Oui! C'est bon!*' somebody said.

'A Remy Martin!'

'Great idea!' I said. (We were all so easily led.)

'It makes a change from wine tasting,' said Lawton.

'*Vive la France! Vive les petits pains! Vive le* Bafana Bafana!'

And so, I am rather ashamed to say, we each sank a Remy Martin. When the bill came for R420 (for just one tot each) our sunburned complexions changed colour as fast as a traffic light. But I discovered, on regaining my composure, that I was able to leap astride my bicycle and with callous disregard for its feelings make it carry me to the top of the hill. For some time afterwards we argued as to whether this spurt of energy was because of the rest, the coffee or the cognac. Our experiments in this interesting psycho-physio-chemico field have continued to this day and I may be offering a paper on the subject to the journal *Science.*

At breakfast one day Didier asked, with great diffidence, if we would mind travelling in the bus to the north-east of Bordeaux and begin cycling again from there. There would be no time, he explained, to get there by bike, see what there was to see, and then get to Bordeaux before dark. He wanted to show us not only two very famous wine estates but he also wanted us to experience one of the finest areas for cycling in Europe – the beginning of the Gironde Estuary formed by the confluence of the Garonne and Dordogne rivers. We readily agreed. It was a Sunday when most chateaux are closed to visitors but Didier had persuaded the Chateau Margaux – a chateau which some would call France's finest producer of red wine (minimum price R1 500 a bottle) – to entertain us.

We parked the bus in a village square and took to our bikes across pleasantly undulating countryside, passing through one or two tiny stone villages and then through a rolling ocean of neat wine estates. Each ridge was surmounted by a terracotta village whose tiny homes huddled around a church like chicks around a hen. The Chateau Margaux is set in elegant grounds and its vineyards cover only 45ha but of the finest soils for producing Bordeaux wine. Not being forewarned we were unable to change into suitable attire for our grand entrance to the elegant château whose staff had been told (we later discovered) that we were 'six eminent editors' from South Africa. Well, that was certainly true of three of my companions but when we saw the staff in their Sunday best lined up on the steps of the imposing neo-classical chateau we felt distinctly like extra-terrestrials and must have looked like them in our gaudy cycling outfits. As I have already observed, cyclists away from their bikes look absurd, especially if wearing those weird streamlined helmets. We managed to pull on our tracksuits which made us feel less bizarre.

Didier introduced us and we were led through the cool, spotless cellars where hundreds of pale wooden barrels were precisely aligned and the wooden cummerbunds around their middles were painted a uniform claret using, instead of paint, the dregs from the grape pressings. A very charming French lass then led us down to a cellar for a wine tasting. As she addressed us we noted a length of fat concertinaed pipe dangling behind her. Harvey, with our Sarlat ducks and their dangling heads in mind, said to us, 'Hey, what does that remind you of?' Our hostess turned around to see what we were looking at and turned a deep crimson. We tried desperately to recover the situation, explaining to her that it reminded us of ceramic ducks, but I could see we were failing miserably. Richard, to change the subject, and taking another sip of a wine that obviously impressed him, asked me what wine I drank at home. I said, 'Swartland Tinta Barocca.' I thought at first he was going to choke. But when I said it tasted a bit like the wine before us, he did choke. I recalled how, a couple of years earlier, a friend had taken me to a formal wine-tasting evening in Johannesburg where I was totally unable to tell an excellent wine from one that was considered *très ordinaire*. Somebody then asked the same question: what wine did I drink at home? I said, 'Swartland Tinta Barocca.' The assembly fell into a shocked silence.

'What's wrong with that?' I asked, a trifle embarrassed.

Finally somebody said, 'It doesn't improve.' I am not one for swift repartee so it was a few days before I realised what I should have said: 'Why should it improve if it tastes good in the first place?'

I asked the vintner at Chateau Margaux how long one should put down a bottle of Bordeaux. He said five to six years: 'There's no point in keeping a red more than eight years.' But when we visited the equally elegant Chateau Pichon-Longueville with its famous turrets capped by pointed roofs, the vintner said 40 years was best for some wines. He asked how long I'd put a good South African red down and I had to confess that wine in my house was like scotch, it doesn't keep. (I have in fact put down South African merlot for eight years but, not knowing what it tasted like at the start, how do I know if it improved?) The Chateau Pichon-Longueville is perhaps the most imposing château in the St-Emilion region and I could see they were very relieved when we declared their wine 'quite excellent'. I even added that it was 'robust' and was about to comment further when Richard silenced me with a crippling tap on the ankle.

St-Emilion itself is a small split-level Romanesque town that once housed 13 000 people but now has only 300. I forget what happened but suspect religious differences, knives, swords and heavy clubs had a lot to do with it. There we trod an ancient cobblestone street that joined the lower part of town to the very touristy but still beautiful upper level. I wondered from where these polished rounded cobbles came for this is limestone country. I doubt there's a naturally occurring cobblestone in the whole of south-west France. The answer was interesting. The 13th century ships that took St-Emilion wine to the English royal court used English river stones as ballast for the return trip and these have been laid along many kilometres of streets in south-western France.

The limestone hill on which the upper town stands is like Emmenthal cheese – full of holes. The ancient cathedral that stands on the hill extends deep below ground its crypt linking up with 200km of tunnels mostly used nowadays for storing wine. In the caves we were shown where the town's founder, Saint Emilion himself, slept – a slab of cold rock. The saint slept on it for decades to demonstrate his love for the Virgin Mary.

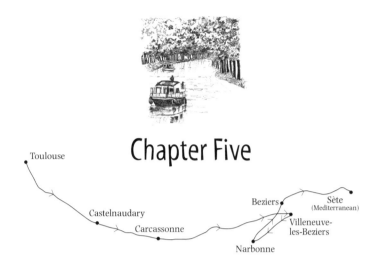

Chapter Five

We spent the night in Bordeaux which we found to be a delightful city with a massive square, some fine buildings and many relics of its Roman beginnings. King Edward – the Black Prince – lived here when the area was under English rule and his son, King Richard II, was born here. And this is where we bade a sad farewell to Didier and to our bikes and took a train to Toulouse.

We were pleasantly surprised by Toulouse and would have liked to have spent more time there. The local tourist department provided us with a guide who heard me say that my favourite food was crab. In her delightful accent she promised, 'I weel tek you were zey serve ze most deleeeshus crebs.' And she led us into a *crêpes* bar. '*Oila!*' she said. We had to admit, French *crêpes* are unrivalled.

Toulouse is what a city should be – full of young people (four universities and 100 000 students) and a large central square filled with activities – even two men in medieval garb fighting with broadswords.

There was great excitement when we arrived because our visit coincided with Munster, a top Irish rugby team, playing Toulouse, a crack French team, that afternoon. As African explorers we were fascinated by the clash of two distinct tribal cultures both addicted to the egg-shaped ball. It ended with the Irish losing after a gargantuan battle and so we witnessed the spectacle of French jubilation and an Irish wake – the flag waving; cars careening in circles with horns blaring; bugles blowing; women dancing in the streets; sad

67

singing about Kathie O'Grady in the bars. We were staying at the same hotel as the Irish team and next morning I commiserated with them. They said it was a great match all the same.

Aviation is a recurring theme in Toulouse. It has an aeronautical and space museum that is unrivalled in Europe. And then there's the Airbus plant on the edge of the city where, in conjunction with the UK, the Concorde was built and where some of the world's top designers are working on tomorrow's generation of jetliners. What interested me about this enormous aircraft establishment – it is Europe's biggest and at that time its sales were overtaking Boeing's – was that the world's first flight in a heavier-than-air machine was made not at Kittyhawk in 1903 but in 1895 at this airfield from where every new Airbus takes off on its delivery run. It didn't perform the required figure of eight achieved by the Wright brothers but its inventor, Clement Ader, at least got it to lift off the ground for 50 metres. With a longer runway the steam-driven bat-like machine would have lifted higher but then, because of fundamental design deficiencies, it certainly would have nose-dived. Nevertheless the French contend Ader was the first human to be lifted off the ground and brought safely back in a heavier-than-air machine which, of course, he was. Many years earlier – in 1871 (32 years before the Wright Brothers' success) – a Frenchman built and flew in Paris a heavier-than-air machine but it was an unmanned model plane. Nevertheless it landed safely and proved that heavier-than-air flying machines capable of transporting people were possible. It was just a matter of scale.

The Wright brothers held centre stage for a very few years before the French again wrested the lead and for many years France dominated the field of aviation – far ahead of the United States and Britain.

I had long been fascinated by the history of aviation and just before *Tour de Farce II* I read of a 'feel-good history book' published mainly for black American children in the state of Washington. Feel-good history is a branch of history where the authors set out to make people feel good about their past. I was taught this kind of history at school in Britain during and after World War II. We were told that the dense 'killer smogs' that settled over Britain in the 1940s and '50s (and killed 6 000 people in December 1952) were a sign of

Britain's industrial might and how this had enabled Britain to buy up whole countries in, for example, Africa, freehold, for vast sums of beads. Sometimes beads were not enough and so quite expensive gunboats had to be used. But as kids we felt good about it, even proud, as we inhaled the soot and the CO_2, SO_2, SO_3 and NOX.

Of course every nation has its own version of history but *African-American Baseline Essays* published by the Portland (Oregon) Public Schools Board, according to many aviation historians, went a bit far in asserting that the first aeroplanes were made in Africa. The assertion was based on a claim that a 14cm model glider had been unearthed somewhere in Egypt and it quoted an obscure authority saying 'the ancient Egyptians used planes for travel expeditions and recreation ...' I have no doubt this is correct. These planes were originally called Pharaoh-planes in honour of the 18th dynasty of Pharaohs who financed their research and development. After the Pharaohs died out the 'ph' was dropped and the machines were simply called 'araoh-planes' and, later, 'aeroplanes' (*Annals of Heavier-than-Air Machines in Egypt*, Tablets III-IV, 3/7/1999BC). A pharaohdrome has been unearthed near Cairo.

The first pharaohplane was developed at Luxor by none other than Damocles Caliph III – it was called the DC3 in his honour. It was known as a heavier-than-air machine on account of it being made from the same type of stone as the Pyramid of Khufu. Many who witnessed the inaugural flight over the Nile's First Cataract thought it was a bird and cried out, 'A swan! A swan!' From this incident the city of Aswan, just below the cataract, derives its name. Eurocentric history books avoid mentioning that Nefertiti began her career as an air hostess with Ancient Egyptian Airlines (*Annals of Ramses II*, 1174 BC, Tablets IV-VII). The general manager was the up-and-coming Tutankhamen (op cit). It is also not widely known that another great Egyptian queen began her career as an airline hostess – Cleopatra herself. Cleopatra eventually founded Cleo's Air Operations – C-AIR-O – the name being eventually adopted by Egypt's capital (sit op). The last Ancient Egyptian Airlines plane to fly had none other than Pontius Pilot at the controls. The plane crashed in the Lower Nile Valley near where the city of A-syut is today. The city's name is derived from Pontius Pilot's last words before he hit the ground. I am not sure how much of this is chronicled in Toulouse's Space and Aeronautical Museum which, alas, we were unable to visit but France's contribution to aeronautics is a reminder that the French have never been short of pioneer scientists and technologists – which brings me back to that amazing feat of engineering, the Canal du Midi. [*Thank goodness for that. Now the reader can appreciate why we spread out on the road. – Ed*]

On the morning we left Toulouse for the main nine-day leg of *Tour de Farce II*, it fell upon me to lead the team out of Toulouse and along the 300-year-old Canal du Midi which passes through the city centre. You can't really miss it. Somehow we did. When, after circling for some time, I found it, the voices in my head said, 'Turn left.'

Sometimes I wish they'd just shut up.

I cycled some distance along the canal path followed by my trusting companions before I felt compelled to ask somebody: '*Pardon moi, monsieur*, is this the way to the Mediterranean?'

Rex remarked, *sotto voce*, 'Thank goodness one of us speaks French!'

The Frenchman said, 'Wee.' Certainly he couldn't have said '*Oui*' because a few kilometres later a signpost pointing to Bordeaux revealed we were heading west instead of east. I had been fooled, not only by the voices and the plughole syndrome and the perversity of a Frenchman, but by the direction in which the canal was flowing. I thought it would be flowing east to the Mediterranean but through Toulouse it flows west back towards the Atlantic. Only later does it miraculously change direction.

[*The author cannot be faulted in this instance. Not by me, anyway. I still cannot sleep at night worrying about why the waters flowed upstream while we were pedalling our way in the opposite direction to reach sea level. The Med cannot be that much higher than the Atlantic, surely? It must be something in the local grapes. – Ed*]

The Canal du Midi, when it was completed in 1681, was the world's most spectacular engineering feat since the Great Wall of China. In 1666, Pierre-Paul Riquet, a native of Béziers – an attractive city through which the canal passes – conceived the idea of linking the Atlantic and Mediterranean by a navigable waterway. It would allow cargo vessels from the Bay of Biscay to take a short cut across France to the Mediterranean. The main part was built in

15 years by 12 000 labourers, of which 600 were women, working with pick and shovel. After the Canal du Midi was built with its 328 tunnels, bridges, dams and locks, workers planted 45 000 plane trees along it. These trees are now huge.

At one point on the canal we cycled along an aqueduct that carries the canal high over the Orb River at Béziers. It was surreal seeing boats chugging high above a river valley. Not far from this point on the Orb the canal – recently listed as a World Heritage Site – descends a steep hill by using a staircase of locks known as the Locks of Fonseranes now a *Monument Historique*. The centuries-old plane trees and cypress trees that line the canal, sometimes on both sides, were planted to provide shade for the horses that towed the cargo boats. Today many of them roof over the entire canal and I can't help paraphrasing Rupert Brooke's *The Old Vicarage, Grantchester*:

> *Oh! There the plane trees, summer through,*
> *Beside the canal make for you*
> *A tunnel of green gloom...*

The reader might assume that following a canal is a bit like following a railway line but not so bumpy and I can hear the reader say that one, surely, cannot possibly get lost following a canal. I can only reply, once again, that I wish the reader would stay out of this. Both assumptions are wrong – very wrong. Certainly the well-surfaced towpath out of Toulouse made for easy cycling and for a time we thought it would be like this all the way. How wrong we were, as I shall shortly explain.

We had a problem in that the bikes we hired in Toulouse had no pannier bags to carry equipment such as cameras, binoculars, rain gear, maps and so on. We were told by the people supplying the bikes that when we reached a village called Montesquieu Lauragais on the canal we could pick up some panniers at the proprietor's house. It would be, they said, a couple of hours' ride. But, after an hour or so of cycling, the voices in my head interrupted my reverie. 'Cough, cough. *Pardon moi*,' they said, 'Do you know the name of the village where you are to pick up the carriers? And do you know where you are staying tonight?' I stopped, dismounted and began patting my pockets looking for the itinerary. Nothing. Our tour instructions –

gone! I patted more and more frantically. My companions gathered around in a circle thinking horseflies were attacking me.

The voices said: 'How are you going to explain to your friends that you've left the itinerary in your luggage and that your luggage is now on its way by taxi to wherever you are staying tonight? You can't even remember the town, can you?'

'No,' I said.

'Nor do you have the foggiest idea of the name of tonight's hotel!'

'You are right,' I said gloomily.

'What,' said the voices, 'are you going to do?'

My companions stood around looking deeply concerned. I think they could hear. I explained to them the situation. There were cries of 'Oh no!' and 'You're kidding!' This was followed by a long silence and much forehead pounding. 'There's no way out,' said Alan as he pulled out his cellphone, 'but to face the humiliation of ringing our wives ...'

He then phoned his wife, Joanne, in Johannesburg and ask her to find the copy of the itinerary he'd left for her and to tell us where we were going. (Our wives had a lot to say about this among themselves, even weeks later. Even years.) She said we were booked into the Hotel du Canal in Castelnaudary, 55km away.

'But what's the name of the village where we're going to pick up the panniers?' asked Lawton. None of us could remember. The name of the village and the name of the bicycle proprietor were also with my luggage. Anyway, I defy anybody to remember a name like Montesquieu Lauragais even for one minute.

We reached the farming community of Montesquieu Lauragais without realising it. There are no signs (mainly, I suspect, because nobody can spell it). Somebody spotted a conspicuous piece of paper tucked in a fence on the canal side. It had my name on it! It turned out to be a *billet doux* (as we linguists say) from the proprietor and it showed precisely how to get to the cycle depot a mere 500m away. Nevertheless we cycled hither and thither doing figures of eight through woods and fields and, in that fine tradition we had developed, we began passing each other coming from different directions. Then we heard distant shouts and saw people beckoning. '*Oila! Ici!* 'Ere!' I had led them to the place.

We gathered from the proprietor that people simply didn't cycle from Toulouse to the Mediterranean. Those who did follow the canal started at Castelnaudary. Even then, they didn't follow the towpath the whole way although, at that stage, we were unable to understand why.

The carriers – the proprietor had only two to spare for the six of us – turned out to be wire shopping baskets that fitted onto the handlebars, the sort that little old ladies use. This presented a serious problem. The canal path was no longer paved and the roots of the ancient plane trees had, over the centuries, invaded the towpath, growing at right angles across it. Cycling along the path was sometimes like riding over railway sleepers. As we bounced along our goods jumped out of the baskets quite high in the air. Our average speed dropped to 8km/h and progress at times was like receiving a sharp kick in the pants every five seconds. At least it shut the voices up. It shut everybody up. We had to clench our teeth to stop the enamel chipping off. It would, somebody shouted, be a permanent cure for piles.

Castelnaudary turned out to be one of those charming little French towns whose streets were lined with grotesquely-pruned plane trees and with a bargain-filled street market where we bought our Treasurer a fanny bag – one of those multi-pocketed leather pouches one wears round one's waist. We thought it would make life easier for him in that he could consider it the *Tour de Farce*'s exclusive bank, but we soon noticed he kept his own money in it too and the kitty was depleting with no less speed than before.

Our hotel was a small, quiet, 19th century place on the canal side and we located it with surprising ease. *Madame la proprietor* viewed us with some amusement but continued with her knitting as if waiting for the *guillotine* to fall. Her smile grew wider as we spoke in what even we recognised as excruciating French and she wordlessly ushered us into the conservatory and presented us with six beers – 'on the 'ouse'. I doubt she knew how much this was appreciated for there had been not a single watering hole on the entire journey. In fact we had averaged that day only 0.34 litres of beer per 100km. [*It was a record economy run – a record we hoped never to break again. – Ed*]

That evening we walked up the street to a restaurant that had been recommended but found it closed. The owner was standing in the doorway, waiting for us, and insisted on driving us to a restau-

73

rant just out of town called *Le Four* ('The Oven') which was owned by his son. We dined on a delicious regional casserole of haricot beans, pork and sausage. It went well with local Corbières wine. The French, of course, could cook cows' horns and still come up with a memorable dish. In three weeks we were never to encounter a mediocre meal – except at Charles de Gaulle Airport where, on the way home, I ordered *confit de canard* for old time's sake and can only conclude that it was an old road kill.

The following day, cycling into a fresh easterly wind, we still had 65km to do. Our destination was Carcassonne, the medieval capital of Aude *département*. At times the canal path, which cuts through undulating countryside, deteriorated into a narrow footpath not much wider than a standard rain gutter. Tree roots across the path became more plentiful. There were no canal side restaurants or even cafés so we made a sortie to a distant village and when we got there, 'there was no there there' (as Dorothy Parker said of somewhere in the Midwest). Not a soul could be found. It was like *The Village of the Damned*. We pedalled 5km back to the canal side.

Depending upon the curve of the canal path the high tunnel formed by the towering plane trees sheltered us from the wind or, at other instances, it became a wind tunnel blowing against us. We became ravenous and I had visions of us resorting to cannibalism. In desperation we again left the canal making for a distant village – Puicheric. It turned out to be as dead as the last. But just as we were about to turn around we spotted an unprepossessing bar. Its bucolic patrons balefully regarded us before dipping their heads back into their beers. I asked the girl behind the bar if she spoke English. '*Non*,' she replied brusquely. I was trying to explain, without sounding too pathetic, that we were seriously hungry and that we would like a sandwich and a beer. She shepherded us like a gaggle of geese into a large, sparsely furnished room with bare boards and bare walls and bid us sit at a long table covered in a plastic cloth.

Sign language is a remarkable thing because she gesticulated that we should sit down and shut up and that we could rest assured that of all the people in the world she and she alone knew exactly what we wanted. Five minutes later she returned with *paté*, salad and bread – and a two-litre lemonade bottle of red wine which, as far as my palate was concerned, could have been a Chateau Margaux blend of Cabernet Sauvignon with perhaps 40 percent Merlot and say 4 percent Cabernet Franc and just a smidgen of Swartland Tinta Barocca with a raspberry aftertaste. We demolished all this with bewildering speed and we all said our heartfelt *'Merci boucoups!'* and *'Délicieux!'* and stuff like that for we were quite overwhelmed by the quality of the food. I asked for the bill but she gestured again, signalling 'sit down and shut up'. A few minutes later she re-entered with six deep soup plates of the most delicious soup, a fresh mound of bread, plus a two-litre Coke bottle of wine. The wine, she made us to understand, was on the house. This we also put away and again I said we'd like to pay but her sign language was louder than mine. Next thing we each had a plate of *cassoulet* placed in front of us and more wine. So we relaxed and began grinning involuntarily. Then came some local cheese and more bread and more wine. The bill was a mere R50 each.

It is difficult to recall the rest of that day's journey. We still had to cover a little over 25km, mostly against a cold headwind. When we reached Carcassonne we were surprised by its size and dismayed by the density of the late-afternoon traffic. The modern part of the city was on one side of the Aude and the greatly elevated older part rose from the opposite bank. As we neared the Aude we saw on a ridge above the river an incredible Camelot-like fortress – the Cité. The sight of this turreted, towered and crenellated medieval fortress – Europe's finest citadel – had us spellbound and we vowed that after a good night's sleep we'd rise early and hire some Sherpas and assault the hill and explore the fortress. I went into a café waving the name of our hotel – the Hôtel Le Donjon-les Remparts – to ask where it was. The dark bar room appeared empty but as my eyes became accustomed to the dark I saw the proprietor drinking coffee with a friend. He surveyed me in my cycling outfit and said in English, 'You look just like Louis Armstrong!'

'You mean Lance Armstrong,' I corrected, adding, 'Louis died long ago.'

'No' he said, 'I meant Louis.'

I asked him for directions to the Hôtel Le Donjon-les Remparts and he gestured to the castle on the hill. Indeed, that's where it was. But we managed to cycle the whole way up and when we got there it was worth every rasping breath. The huge fortress has but one heavily fortified entrance protected by a drawbridge – an idea I pass on, gratis, to future Johannesburg cluster-home developers. Inside its battlements live 1 000 people and our luxurious hotel was a cleverly converted Dark Age residence with a fantastic chef. (I later learned that the fortress was in fact extensively renovated for the film *Camelot*.)

We were invited to a pre-prandial wine tasting at the Cellier des Vignerons in one of the narrow cobbled streets. Its elegant proprietor, Christine, began by serving Limoux and we all made appreciative noises. I had become quite good at looking as if I knew whether a wine was presumptuous or well rounded. Then came a local Languedoc Chardonnay over which we enthused. Then a seriously outstanding red from St Chinian; then, I think, a wine from nearby Minervois. I cannot make much sense of my notes after this. In truth I find all wine pleasant, except retsina. Retsina tastes like a grizzly bear's early-morning urine sample after six months of hibernating.

[*There appear to be no limits to the talents of the Leader of the Tour de Farce. Nor any accounting for his tastes. He omitted to mention, for instance, the succulent, unpronounceable confections which the Stuckes had introduced us to in the Dordogne Valley. We called the sweets 'honey-balls', for that is what they were – balls of honey held together in a delicate glacé of beeswax and maple syrup. They tasted good even with beer. Our Leader has also failed to mention the world's best* paté de foie gras *which we sampled along the Dordogne. I suspect because he can't spell it. We were led by our guide to its home-ground, where we were transfixed by a display of viands mostly concerned with duck too delicious to describe. Regrettably, the look on the face of the ceramic duck, looking down forlornly from my bookshelf, disturbs the memory of that elegant feast. – Ed*]

The site on which the Cité is built has been occupied for 2 500 years and it commands a view of a countryside that has witnessed the most terrible Middle Age atrocities. Muslims massacred people who did not believe in Mohammed; Christians slaughtered people who didn't believe in Christ and then they fell upon even those who did. In nearby Béziers Catholics murdered non-Catholics and, on a productive day, if everybody skipped lunch, they were able to kill up to 20 000 people. When they reported to the Pope's emissary that they found they had, by mistake, killed Catholics he told them to carry on because God would sort them out at the other end.

Today blood still splashes onto the region's fields for the locals play very competitive rugby.

Early in the morning, despite there being so much more to see at Carcassonne (we even had to miss the dungeons) we felt it prudent to start off early. The wind was still against us and our backsides had taken a terrible pounding on the tree roots the day before. The canal path became more and more corrugated and in places became overgrown so we took to the country lanes keeping, all the time, the line of trees along the canal in view. The roadsides revealed brilliant bursts of colour from daffodils and poppies.

Harvey remarked: 'It's hard to imagine a more relaxing pastime than cycling on a spring day in the sunny French countryside knowing that at the end of the day there's a comfortable hotel and a great dinner booked in our names!'

'Sheer *joie de vivre!*' said Richard.

Rex said, 'I bet the French have an expression for that?'

On May Day we entered Serignan and noticed the French Communist Party was holding a rally. Only three people had turned up with, curiously, an old Soviet flag. I felt like consoling them with the news that in Africa there were still lots of people who believed in communism *à la* the defunct Soviet Union.

Our next night's stop was Villeneuve-les-Béziers – a beautiful annex of Béziers, the town where the builder of the canal, Pierre Riquet lived. Looking for La Chamberte, our hostelry for the night, we found the street easily enough but not even the neighbours knew the address we were seeking. We had to phone the proprietor on a cellphone and he said "ang on', then, like a genie out of a bottle, he popped out of a wall right next to us. He was wearing a singlet and very brief floral shorts. Hands a-flutter he surveyed us and, giggling, said, '*Oila!*' Translated, he meant 'What 'ave we 'ere? Venusians?' We asked him why he didn't have a sign outside and he told us that he and his partner (an architect) did not like people to know about their place because they didn't want riffraff. My companions all glanced at me.

It was a most stunning and unusual house and it had an equally stunning restaurant that people book for weeks ahead. The regional tourist authority had thoughtfully booked for us and the dinner was superb. La Chamberte is at 4, Rue de la Source, Villeneuve-les-Béziers – but you didn't get that from *moi*, OK?

Next day we began to worry about Rex. After 10 days of cycling it transpired that he was having serious conversations with his bum. He was suffering because, despite the ingenious designs available, the modern bicycle saddle and the gluteus maximus muscles are not good friends. The professionals use saddles no larger than a samosa while we had saddles like tractor seats but one can still get sore. Rex made no fuss but we could see he was suffering. In my pep talk at dinner that night I said that his stoicism reminded me of Captain Oates in the 1912 Antarctic expedition with Scott when his gangrenous foot became a frozen block and he realised he was slowing down the others. With the words, 'Gentlemen, I may be gone some time', he gallantly walked out of the tent into the howling blizzard, never to be seen again. We feared Rex might be tempted to cycle into the Canal du Midi saying something similar over his shoulder. Instead he announced in a voice that brooked no argument, 'Gentlemen, I have promised my bum a cycle-free day tomorrow.'

Fortunately we were entering the Roman city of Narbonne through which the beautiful Canal du Rhone passes looking like a serious river. It so happened we were due to spend two nights here. Thus we were able to explore on foot Ancient Rome's first colonial garrison. It proved to be the highlight of our travels. We trod a recently discovered section of the Roman road in the city centre, its cobblestones still bearing the scars of chariot wheels and the polish from the sandals of generations of Romans and Gauls. Harvey and I sat against a wall in the 13th century cathedral of St Just, overawed by the Gothic pillars soaring the equivalent of seven storeys to hold up Europe's second-highest cathedral roof. The place was filled with ghosts. Somewhere, unseen, an organ was playing softly. Shafts of sunlight slanted down from the high windows of the unfinished building – unfinished because to have built the remainder would have meant destroying the adjacent city wall. It was just as well they didn't because that wall later stopped the Black Prince and his army invading the town.

Out of respect for Rex's bum we sat only at outdoor cafés that had padded seats. We found ourselves surrounded by medieval street scenes. The slow-moving cars seemed out of place. It was like sitting in the past witnessing the future.

Early on the day of our departure we were met by a guide who turned out to be a very beautiful girl named Annie whose enchanting accent and dazzling smile had us all holding in our stomachs. Annie led us back to Béziers along the route the Romans used to penetrate the rest of Gaul. We jostled in a most unseemly manner to cycle alongside her and to charm her with our wit and fathomless depths of knowledge. As we followed the barely discernible Roman road – more of a footpath now – across a grassy meadow, a spooky old farm loomed ahead. Annie stopped and we all nearly crashed into her. She told us there were two Baskerville-like hounds at the farm and she was petrified of them. As titular leader of the *Tour de Farce* I instructed my five companions to fan out in front of Annie while I watched her rear. This worked splendidly. Disappointingly the dogs did not appear.

Next day we reached the Mediterranean. We began by leisurely traversing the coastal wetlands through which the canal passes. It's not particularly attractive country and became less attractive as we reached the last bridge over the 340km-long canal and headed dead north to the commercial port of Sète where the Canal du Midi ends. Before us was an 18km-long busy road running between trailer homes on one side and a narrow, gritty beach on the other. Sète is a rather dull place and knowing what we know now we should have arranged to continue to cycle along a differently named canal leading beyond Sète to the quaint little town of Arle – an easy day's ride away. Arle, which I had visited twice before, is where Van Gogh and Gauguin painted for a time. In fact where the former cut off his ear. South of Arle is a beautiful coastal wilderness – the Camargue with its wild horses. Alas, we had other commitments.

We abandoned our bikes in a hotel basement and it did not escape my attention that Rex kicked his machine before leaving it.

It is interesting to see other people's attitudes towards bikes. While in France we read that a young Swede had just cycled the full length of Europe. When I say a Swede I do not mean the large white vegetable like a mutant radish, I mean Patrik Ahlvik of Stockholm who, on a heavy Post Office bicycle with sit-up-and-beg handlebars cycled from Norway's North Cape 1 450km to Gibraltar – and back. Ahlvik told reporters, 'It is a very special feeling to live with a bicycle for five months.' Indeed, I at least can confirm that one becomes very attached to one's bike. One feels very reassured when, at dawn, you get up and see your faithful trek bike patiently leaning against a wall ready to carry you onwards. I called my bike Cynthia-Anne and over the days I grew very fond of her and, I like to think, Cynthia-Anne grew fond of me. If I caught any of the others so much as touching her my hair would stand on end, making it difficult to keep my helmet on. When we finally parted with our bikes in that dark basement in Sète I asked my companions to leave me alone with Cynthia-Anne while I explained to her why I had to return to Africa without her.

Richard said I should see a specialist.

[*The author is a fickle cycle-lover. He forgets about our first loves – those broad-beamed, virginal, unrattled, totally reliable bikes we were given in Passau. Beautiful they were, and as strong as Hungarian potato-pickers. We abandoned them in Vienna halfway through our 1 000 journey down the Danube. I still worry about them. So should the author. But, as you will discover later in this narrative, he was soon to get his leg-over an Irish bike, slender as a filly … and it threw him, badly! – Ed*]

We ended our three-week tour by catching a train to Montpellier, a sunny, cheerful university city 30km inland whose outstanding feature is Comédie Square – a huge, traffic-free, tiled square encircled by cafés and alive with students. Clean, litter-free Comédie Square is the sort of square every city should have. Montpellier was a fitting place to end an African expedition traversing the remote south-west corner of Gaul.

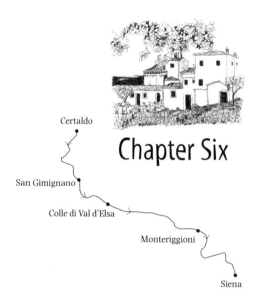

Certaldo

San Gimignano

Colle di Val d'Elsa

Monteriggioni

Siena

Chapter Six

In August 2004 we held a meeting to plan a cycle ride clean across Italy – after all, it's a nice thin country.

That year our average age dropped dramatically from 70 down to 66 – sadly, Lawton (72) had had to drop out because of clashing overseas engagements and Peter Sullivan, aged 55 – current group editor in chief of Independent Newspapers – replaced him. This meant we were much younger now and, therefore, more agile and could do things that people in their 70s should never even attempt.

We had chosen Italy because, having experienced the gastronomic delights of France, we felt that in the interests of objective international cuisineology we had a duty to try Italy's fabled food.

At the meeting Harvey raised a serious doubt. He feared Italian wine would not give us sufficient calorific boost and that we were unlikely to get more than 30km per litre out of it. It is Harvey's nature to issue finger-wagging warnings and I, as leader of this expedition, was bound to heed them because Harvey was, by virtue of having lived so long, the team's health adviser. In 2003 when *Tour de Farce II* sped across south-west France we had managed quite well on Bordeaux wine and *les grand vins du* Languedoc Roussillon.

Harvey said he had experimented and had worked out that even consuming an occasional glass of South African wine would barely contain enough sugar to keep us going for any useful distance. 'And what will we get out of Chianti?' he asked. [*I later mused that a lower octane wine might prove to be a boon – a light, chuckling Chianti could mean more stops to fuel up; more time to philosophise about the really important things in life such as rugby and food and Richard's plughole theory. – Ed*]

I had, in the meantime, heard from The Skittles, a group of mothers who lived in northern Johannesburg and had taken up cycling. Although we've never seen them in action the formidable Skittles ride sleek, drop-handle, state-of-the-art racing bikes and no doubt wear designer cycling togs. By contrast, our all-male *Tour de Farce* team rides sit-up-and-beg, state-of-the-Ark mountain bikes which have everything except a piece of stiff cardboard sticking into the back spokes to go clack-a-de-clack-a-de-clack. (Not that we haven't thought of doing this.) Sue Stricker of The Skittles had e-mailed in response to my airing, in my column, the question of how many kilometres per litre of wine we were likely to achieve during our tour of Italy's richest wine region – Tuscany and Umbria, which includes the Chianti region. The Skittles, it turned out, have a depth of knowledge and experience regarding wine as well as cycling because three of them own wine farms in the Cape. They are serious cyclists and although they don't take themselves seriously they regularly cycle 25km before driving their daughters to school at 7 am. In Sue's e-mails she convinced me that one would get more kilometres per litre out of South African wine than out of Chianti. When I raised this at the meeting Harvey's finger again wagged and he said that on that evidence wine must obviously be a performance- enhancing substance and, strictly speaking, we should eschew it. Alan said that if wine is a performance-enhancing substance then how about beer or even Coca-Cola or bananas? That's the thing about cycling, it stimulates the brain and one has these deep intellectual debates. Rex said all wine and beer, when one considers their natural sugar content, were performance-enhancing substances. 'Water is also a performance-enhancing agent when you come to think about it,' he said. There followed a long silence as we thought about drinking water.

We learned that one of The Skittles, Barbie 'Puller' May earned her sobriquet because, being the strongest cyclist, she 'pulls' the others along in her slipstream. Ye gods! The Skittles suggested that as I was the weakest rider I should position myself behind the rest. The thought of the *Tour de Farce* team pulling me along in its wake – or even disturbing a toffee paper lying in the road – was beyond my imagination.

I mentioned to my colleagues that a FAQ (frequently asked question) from readers of my column was: How far do we cycle on an average day? Reader Clive Urquart asked, 'Lance Armstrong averages almost 50km an hour. What about you?' This triggered a longer silence because 50km is sometimes all we achieve in a day although, seriously, we could manage fairly comfortably 100km a day on the open road. Peter wondered whether we shouldn't aim to cover longer distances and perhaps pedal *down* the length of Italy instead of merely across it. There was no response to this save a gasp or two and, as Leader, I let the matter drop. Nevertheless it was nice to hear such youthful enthusiasm.

During the meeting, one or two members had mentioned there would be a lot of uphill work cycling through Tuscany and Umbria. The very mention of the word 'uphill' inevitably caused much groaning and eyeball rolling. I try to avoid even using the word 'hill' in front of the lads. I hopefully suggested that should we find 'any extreme elevation occurring in the topography' we could dismantle our bikes and get on a bus until we reached the point where the route begins going downhill. At the mention of the word 'downhill' some members of the team released little involuntary noises. After far too short a discussion regarding buses my idea was thrown out.

Peter, whose cycling ensemble includes a sky-blue wide-brimmed hat held down by his silver Bell helmet and, often, a long black shirt and black shorts, looks like the follower of a religious sect that worships woodlice. Apart from his eccentricities regarding dress he is frequently seized by eccentric ideas and prefaces them all by exclaiming 'Hey!' 'Hey!' he said. 'Why not invite Lance Armstrong to join us?' Richard said Armstrong could never keep up with us because part of our mission was to sample local cuisine and, he had noted, not a single cyclist in the 2004 *Tour de France* had bothered to stop – not even for lunch or even for a beer. 'Did you ever see Armstrong looking around at the scenery?' he asked. 'Did any of them stop to smell the roses?' There was another long silence broken only by the sound of shaking heads.

I had to remind the meeting that our primary mission was not to break records or vie for King of the Mountains. Our mission was to avoid mountains and, *inter Italia* as they say in Italy, try to bring back the seeds of that country's mysterious spaghetti tree – *Pastaritus yumitums*. We were also hoping to pioneer a route, navigable by aged cyclists, from the Tyrrhenian Sea to the Adriatic via Tuscany and Umbria, something that even Marco Polo never achieved.

I read out another FAQ: 'Are you all mad?'

This led to a still longer silence and when I woke up everybody had gone home. I then declared the meeting closed.

By now the wide-awake reader will have gathered that with our tours we liked to do something explicit. Like cycle *down* the Danube and *across* France. We liked to achieve something geographically precise just as Captain Scott tried to do when he aimed for the South Pole or Edmund Hillary and Tenzing Norgay did when they clambered *up* Everest instead of simply playing around on its side. In 2004 we had been confronted with the choice of either crossing India (not only by bike, of course, but by various forms of transport) or of crossing Italy. The team chose to cross Italy not only because it was a lot thinner, but mainly because India would require much more time and a great deal more planning than some of us could afford in 2004.

My readers, on hearing of the Italian expedition, had many helpful suggestions. Sam Mkhuma of Newcastle in Natal wrote, 'Don't forget to keep right!' Diana McCutcheon of Polokwane, on reading that we were considering bringing back to South Africa the mysterious seeds of the *Pastaritus yumitums* (an idea we eventually dropped) usefully informed us that it belonged 'to the family *Farinaceae* along with the breadfruit tree and muffin bush. As is the case with nutmeg and mace, which come from a single tree, she informed us that spaghetti and macaroni also come from a single tree species. The macaroni forms the outer layer of the fruit which, when stripped off, reveals the inner core which is called 'spaghetti' ('spag' meaning inner and 'hetti' meaning 'core'.) Diana believed the seeds were available under the name of 'rice noodles' but she could have been kidding. She said she wasn't sure when the spaghetti tree came into flour. This, I might say, is typical of the sort of help and advice we so received and for which we were truly grateful.

TUSCANY

TOP: Looking surprisingly chipper after having flown throughout the night from South Africa to Dubai, then on to Rome, the team awaits a train in Florence. CENTRE Certaldo in upper Tuscany, seen from our hotel. BELOW LEFT: Cycling down a farm road – a strada bianca (white road). BELOW RIGHT: Nobody was ever more deserving of a beer than I was at this stage.

Tour de Farce III – Italy: Tuscany

TOP: The team about to set off from Certaldo. The new man, Peter Sullivan, second from left.
FAR LEFT: The Leader found a child's fairy wand and changed Rex's bike into a smaller model – Rex not terribly impressed.
CENTRE: A Montelcino policewoman (she was in high heels) with arresting looks. LEFT: Richard Steyn.
BELOW: The 700-year-old Ponte Vecchio – the only Florentine bridge left standing after World War II.

Tour de Farce III – Italy: Tuscany

Taking in the sights of Florence can induce 'Stendhal's syndrome' – a recognised neurotic reaction (dizziness, even fainting) caused by trying to absorb too much of Florence in one go. TOP LEFT: Our hardened photographer's sneaked picture of David. (David's pecker had to be shortened because the city fathers said it made them feel inadequate.) TOP: Admiring Lorenzo Ghiberti's 'Gate of Paradise' on the east doors of Florence's Baptistry – just before Stendhal's syndrome kicked in. LEFT: Front door of the Duomo.

Tour de Farce III – Italy: Tuscany

TOP: Like meerkats who've just seen a martial eagle – we were pondering over direction (as usual). Harvey and Rex defeated by a gradient. CENTRE: The Leaning Tower of Pisa where we had a pizza in a pizzeria in a piazza next to a Pisa palazzo. INSET: Leonardo Simonelli-Santi, aristocratic wine and olive grower and owner of the Hotel Palazzuolo in San Quirico d'Orcia. Above him, the entrance to his village. RIGHT: The dreadful beach at Maremma National Park.

Tour de Farce III – Italy: Tuscany

TOP: Our photographer has no idea where this was. CENTRE: A Tuscan vineyard viewed from Monteriggioni. BELOW RIGHT: Pienza's warm stonework. BELOW LEFT: San Gimignano – a medieval Manhattan that used to bristle with 75 towers, now has only 15.

Tour de Farce III – Italy: Tuscany

UMBRIA

TOP: We found every downhill was followed by an uphill. INSET: This was a typical result – Rex in repose. CENTRE: The scene after our first and only roadside picnic. LEFT: A study in triangles – Peter Sullivan (who tended to be hyperactive) arranged us in this pyramidal grouping.

Tour de Farce III – Italy: Umbria

Three pilgrims – Alan, Harvey and Rex outside the Upper Church of the Basilica of St Francis which was badly damaged in the 1997 earthquake. BELOW: To the right is the entrance to the crypt where the bones of Italy's favourite saint are buried.

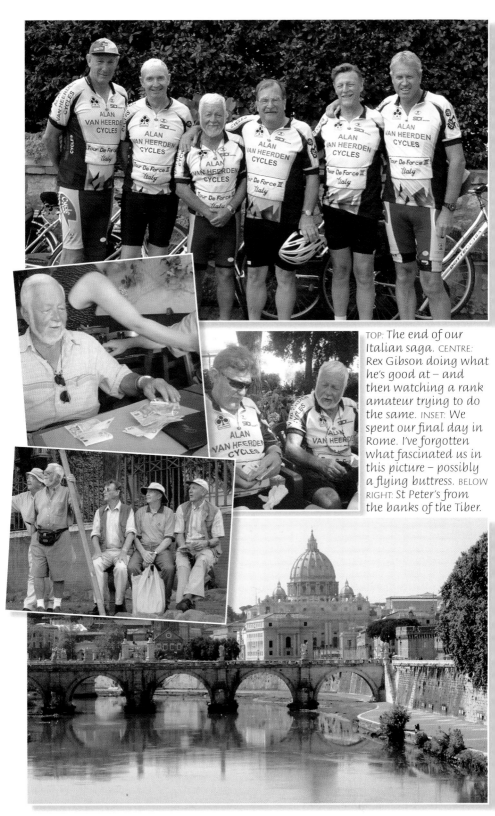

TOP: The end of our Italian saga. CENTRE: Rex Gibson doing what he's good at – and then watching a rank amateur trying to do the same. INSET: We spent our final day in Rome. I've forgotten what fascinated us in this picture – possibly a flying buttress. BELOW RIGHT: St Peter's from the banks of the Tiber.

Tour de Farce III – Italy: Umbria

Help regarding cycle routes was hard to find among the corridors of Italian bureaucracy and, after two months without a response from ENIT, the state tourism board in Rome (I needed information about existing cycling routes and the possibility of mapping one across central Italy), I e-mailed ENIT's London bureau and received an immediate reply from Alessandra Smith, press officer. The Lower Tuscany Tourist Board also proved very helpful indeed. However the most obliging, useful and immediate source of expertise was Serena Cartwright in Cape Town who turned out to be the wife of a former colleague, Tim Cartwright, son of the author, AP 'Paddy' Cartwright, who, coincidentally, was a predecessor of Rex as editor of the *Rand Daily Mail*. Serena virtually became our agent, for she represented a number of overseas cycling companies including ATG Oxford which organises cycling and hiking trails throughout Europe. Thus we were able to plan our route through Serena and pay in South African rands which made life much simpler.

During this time I found some advice on long-distance cycling by Ellie Bennett, a South African athlete who said that while cycling she 'listens to her own body'. Lance Armstrong said something similar about listening to voices from within. This came as no surprise because I have always listened to my body when cycling – the wheezing of the lungs; the rhythmic arthritic clicks; the rumbling sounds of my inner self as we near a village and catch the aroma of freshly baked bread. As for listening to voices from within – I never ignore them. If I try to ignore them they can get so loud that people around me hear them too.

'Look! Look!' the voices cry. 'A quaint wayside inn! Let us hither hence that we may replenish our carbon levels and thus cycle on with renewed vigour!'

'But we've only done 3km since the last stop!' says another voice of the inner variety.

'Why don't you shut up?' says the first.

'Who are you telling to shut up?'

'Who d'ya think, you stupid git?'

'Yeah?'

'Yeah!'

Sometimes I have to pull my helmet down over my ears for fear my companions will overhear all this nonsense.

We had to postpone *Tour de Farce III* until September which we were assured was an ideal time for cycling through Tuscany and Umbria. These regions are situated just above Italy's kneecap. It is the time of year when the harvest is reaped and the vines are at their peak and the nut-brown Italian maidens start hitching up their skirts to tread the grapes to the buoyant rhythm of Italian music. (I just hope they wash their feet.) Certainly the farmers would be seeking our expert opinion on the season's young wines which, of course, we would freely give just as we had been able to give encouraging advice to the staff at various chateaux in France.

Once again I found myself in training – striding out at dawn, scattering the sparrows, leaping streams and vaulting quite high walls. The postponement gave me time to become fluent in Italian and learn useful phrases such as '*Sixo piazzas, multi grassaggio!*' (Six pizzas, thank you very much.) As leader it was incumbent upon me to act as interpreter as I had done in France where – and I say this with all due modesty – many people remarked on my French, mostly by saying things like 'What?' But, as I observed earlier, it is one thing to learn how to ask a question in a foreign language but quite another to know what anybody says in reply. For example, you may ask the way to the bank ('*Punto banco, pliza?*') and somebody might reply, '*Le gengive mi sanguinano!*' and where would that leave you? For all you know they could be telling you their gums are bleeding. The Italian language is particularly difficult and can easily lead to serious misunderstanding. Look where it got Mussolini. And Caesar. Galileo too – Galileo spent years in jail just for saying something about the sun. Clearly it is safer to stick to simple pleasantries such as, '*Buon guano.*'

The Italians are funny people. Their young women are, to my eye, more beautiful and elegant than any in Europe but one has to catch them before they get to 40 when they start sprouting RAF moustaches. [*This statement may prove troublesome when the T de F launches another expedition into Italy. – Ed*] Italian men are noisy and macho but have the reputation of making poor soldiers. When Italy entered World War II on Germany's side somebody rushed into Winston Churchill's office and said, 'Italy has just joined the Germans!'

Churchill said, 'It's only fair. We had them last time.'

[*To be fair, the Italians for about a thousand years were great fighters, even after they began paying others to do it for them. When they had finally tried every form of warfare and every form of rule – from horse-consuls to dictatorships and communism – they tried to give up practising both war and government. – Ed*]

Before we could formally agree to Peter joining us we felt obliged, because of his age, to ask him to furnish us with a letter from his mother to say he could ride a two-wheeler and that he could stay up after 10 pm. Alan felt that as Peter was so much younger and fitter – despite a life-and-death emergency heart operation three years earlier – he should somehow be handicapped on the tour. Rex, who has a cruel side, suggested removing his saddle.

To welcome Peter to the team we decided to have a joint training session in preparation for Italy –a spaghetti and vino dinner at a local Italian restaurant. We came away quite pleased with our performance. As expedition Leader I was allowed to preside over the dinner and settle the bill. This, Richard said in a brief vote of thanks, was a privilege that naturally fell upon a leader. In a longer speech I thanked them all for the honour and expressed my delight in their continued confidence in my leadership for which I received prolonged applause.

Harvey raised an interesting point. He drew attention to how professional we were going to look to the casual observer in our new cycling livery – white shirts emblazoned with the words 'Alan van Heerden Cycles' and, below, '*Tour de Farce III* – Italy'. He pointed out how it might become embarrassing when we got to a steep hill and our coffee-grinder breathing began to disturb other road users and, one by one, we toppled exhausted from our bikes and resorted to pushing them. It would be even more embarrassing when other cyclists flashed past and our caps were whisked off our heads in their slipstreams. Alan suggested we carry overcoats and gumboots and put them on whenever we pushed our bikes up hills so that passing cyclists would think we were local ploughmen plodding our weary way o'er the lea. Rex said there are little motors made for bicycles and if we had any sense we'd buy them. Harvey said that would be even more humiliating.

Coping with ageing

It was clear that my two older companions, Harvey and Rex, were worried about the increasing manifestations of ageing. Personally I think too much is made of ageing and of the slow decline of the body and mind. Certainly one becomes grumpier but that is perfectly understandable – and, yes, it becomes increasingly difficult to control one's prejudices, especially against other races, other nationalities, the opposite sex, other drivers, Maltese terriers, computers, the public service and the young. This is all perfectly natural and I have no problem with it for it stems from the fact that one has now acquired what younger people lack – wisdom and vast knowledge.

The young become especially irritating. This is because every day there are more and more people younger than you telling you what to do. Many of them don't seem to realise that when a journalist, particularly a male journalist, passes middle age he knows more or less everything. True, I do not understand DOS, but neither did Leonardo da Vinci and he was pretty bright. And I'll admit too that I don't understand how it is that my secretary, Threnody, has fish swimming across her PC screen as a screensaver. I don't even know how she puts the water in – and I daren't ask. But I know everything else.

When I walk into a big office these days, it pains me to see young people, considerably less knowledgeable than me (and often not even white or male) elevated to positions that in my day only grey-haired white men held. Like editorships. Wherever one turns nowadays, there are younger and younger people in control. One gets on a plane and there's a fresh-faced youngster, hardly old enough to shave, wearing a uniform and you realise he is your captain and he is going to lift 256 tons of aeroplane – carrying enough people to fill the average town hall – 10km up in the sky while the air hostesses take turns sitting on his knee. I feel equally uncomfortable when faced with a surgeon who was not even born when I was old enough to be running around gathering bad news for my newspaper and yet he is about to stick a knife into my person. Yet there it is – one is forced to hand over to people who are clearly less clever than oneself, who never knew hardship, who never had to walk to school in blizzards pursued by hungry wolves or work 18 hours a day down a coal pit for 20c a week. Worst of all, you constantly have to ask the kid across the road to tell you what's wrong with your C7000 Kripton-argon New Age Flashwriter PC – and he laughs at it.

'Ha ha ha ha ha. It's from the Olden Days, man! It hasn't even got a 576/99 Silicon zipperjet.'

'What do you mean, "Olden Days"?'

'Like the dinosaur, man!'

'Dinosaur?'

'Like, it's from the 1980s! The reason it won't go is because it isn't plugged in.' He switches it on.

'Thank you, little kid. Here, take this.'

Whop!

'Waaaaaaaaaaaaaaaaaaaa!'

The art of doddering

One of Peter's problems – and it became more and more apparent as we went along – was that he had not yet learned to dodder. Doddering is a virtue that comes with age. Peter would make snap decisions that would often make some of us jump. I constantly had to tell him to dodder down a bit. He was sometimes impatient when, say, at a T-junction the five of us older and more experienced cyclists would come up with five different opinions as to which direction to take. I recall an evening in France – before Peter joined us – when we happily wandered round Toulouse for two hours trying to decide at which restaurant to eat only to end up back at our hotel in a state of collapse. That's how it was with us.

Another of Peter's problems was that he leads a very full life and is full of party-stoppers. We might be discussing some of the grim battles we had had with our personal computers and he would say, 'When I was having lunch with Bill Gates in New York last week I mentioned this very problem ...' or 'as I said to Ronald Reagan in the Oval Office ...' The fact is that he operates at this level. Being a journalist I also have this compulsive desire to interrupt with party-stoppers and name-dropping. I once shook hands with Prince Charles. But it takes a high level of alertness and timing to pick an appropriate gap in a conversation where it becomes relevant to say, 'I once shook hands with Charles.' It could in fact fall flat. There was also the time I met Diana Dors ... but who really cares? Peter would

89

have said it reminded him of the time he had a stand-up fight with Jane Fonda (which he did).

It was back to training.

One morning while I was cycling round my complex a jogger and Comrades Marathon runner, Gerry de Boer, caught up with me on a hill and pushed me along in front of him. I told him, with some conviction, that cycling was more healthy than jogging. For a start the brain is not churned like butter by the jarring that comes with jogging. The brain, while cycling, remains undisturbed like porridge left to cool – unless, of course, one is cycling on a cobbled road; then indeed it does tend to slop around a bit. The bike I keep at home is a placid old mountain bike and, like its registered owner, it is not built for speed. It has tyres like a Massey Ferguson. I bought it because mountain bikes are more suitable for what Richard has aptly labelled 'coarse cycling'. They are cheaper and more robust than those bikes made for 'fine cycling' that have drop handlebars and tyres so thin that Oxfam workers try to feed them. It's not that I ever envisaged cycling up mountains. Far from it. Though, I must say, the hills where I now live are pretty steep and in my daily circuit I climb high into the tundra. In fact the entire route, circular though it is, is uphill, or so it seems.

The beauty of cycling in my enclosed neighbourhood is that one seldom gets run over. But there's the problem of greeting people. The year we went to Italy I moved to a bigger suburban fortress of 1 000 houses and when cycling two or three times round its 5km circumference early in the morning one can, hypothetically, pass the same jogger or walker three times or, if one has had one's porridge before setting out, even four times and one forgets to whom one has said 'Good morning'. One feels a right ninny greeting somebody three times in half an hour. At the same time, if you fail to greet them the word gets round that you are a grumpy old sod. The only solution is to squirt people with a dye once you have greeted them.

Tough times in Tuscany

We set off for Italy in September 2004 and, to save money, flew via Dubai. It turned out to be the equivalent of flying halfway round the fattest part of the world – an eight-hour flight to Dubai (arriving in the small hours) followed by six hours to Rome. And the money we saved was absorbed by buying coffee and a croissant at Dubai airport. So perhaps it was sheer fatigue that led to our confusion on arrival in Rome. At the central station, considering we were all seasoned travellers, we had the devil's own job finding the train to Florence. We were due to change at Florence for Certaldo, the starting point of our cycle ride. The Italian rail system does not make things easy for foreigners. In fact we were often left with the impression that the Italians actively dislike visitors and would much rather we stayed at home and posted them money.

While I stayed with the luggage the other five set off in different directions on intelligence-gathering missions. One found that the train to Florence was leaving from Platform 1, two said it was from 4 and a fourth was told Platform 9. As two concurred on Platform 4 that is where we went. There we found an Italian family who assured us we were on the right platform and pointed to the indicator screen which read 'Firenze' (Florence). It worried us though that there were so few people yet the train was imminent. With only five minutes to go the family suddenly panicked and ran off into the distance shouting '*Sette!*' (Seven!) We hurtled along in their wake and were just in time to leap aboard the train. Thank goodness, I thought, that Peter had reduced our average age to well below 70 because we could never normally have run that fast with our luggage.

The train sped through countryside that was bathed in autumn sunshine and it seemed that every other hill wore a crown in the shape of a medieval citadel. As the express hummed along and the blue-grey olive groves and lush vineyards slid past, some of us dozed off. Harvey and Rex who, having first driven from Hermanus to Cape Town and then flown to Johannesburg before flying to Dubai and then on to Rome had by now been travelling for 28 hours.

We reached Certaldo late in the afternoon and stepped out of the station sweaty and unshaven to survey the town's steep Via San Giugno leading up to the base of the centuries-old fortified upper town – Certaldo Alto. That's where our hotel was situated – at the highest point. Although there is a funicular it meant a 500m walk to get to it so we hired two taxis for the 1km drive through the maze of narrow cobbled streets.

After booking into the 400-year-old Hotel Vicario Osteria we were supposed to turn left out of the front door and walk down the street to our rooms but something made us turn right. Call it a sixth sense, if you like, but we did it with our instinctive finch-like flocking motion. In retrospect it was probably because there was no sign of a café or bar down the hill and we were seriously dehydrated. Around the corner we saw – and I will try not to be too sentimental about it – one of the most beautiful sights in Tuscany. Nay, in the whole of Europe at the time. We found ourselves in a 13th century piazza and, on an iron table in a shady corner, a shaft of sunshine was beaming down on an object of singular beauty – an enormous glass of golden beer. We flopped into chairs and ordered one each – our first Italian draft beer. It came in a litre-sized mug and a minute or two later we were staring into our empty glasses. Well, at least, I was.

Later, too tired to change the clothes we had worn from South Africa and having decided on an early night, we wondered down a steep and narrow alley to a delightful restaurant where we sat on a terrace with a panoramic view of Upper Tuscany. In the valley below were Roman walls and tiled roofs. Far to the south, high on a hill was a citadel toothier with medieval towers than any we'd seen up to now – San Gimignano, our destination the day after tomorrow.

Some of us ordered wild boar. Remembering how the Ancient Romans had tried to domesticate Africa's guinea fowl I ordered that. It was excellent. Everything was excellent and we joined in some banter with an English family at the next table.

It was a clear, warm evening and, as the sun slowly set, the lights of distant villages competed with the stars. We raised our glasses to Italy and toasted a lot of other things besides. Even our wives. Alan suggested we send them flowers on the morrow. The silence that followed was broken by Rex who said with his usual gravity, 'Never do anything that might vaguely suggest to those at home that we might be feeling even a tiny bit guilty about being here without them.' We solemnly raised our glasses to our Treasurer's unquestionable wisdom.

We agreed that as we had the whole of the next day to spare we would get a train back to Florence and spend the day there.

Culture shock

There's a name for it – Stendhal's syndrome. In Florence we displayed all the symptoms. We were standing outside the Galleria dell'Accademia in Florence in the hot noonday sun, reeling from the shock of finding how expensive it was to go in – especially as the only thing that really interested us in the gallery was the world's most famous statue – Michelangelo's David sculpted in 1504. There are a few replicas in Italy but this was the original sculpted when Michelangelo was 29. Harvey was pretty sure he'd seen the original some years back when it was still standing in the open. Richard said this was quite possible because it was moved indoors only in 1874.

Peter was impatient to go in but we were content to dodder, especially as just up the road we had spotted a small restaurant that served beautifully balanced pizzas and, being lunchtime, we were weak with hunger. The question was, said Rex as Keeper of the Purse, should we or shouldn't we blow R800 from our kitty to see David? We had been arguing about it for much longer than sensible people should when Harvey tried to lighten the whole thing by emerging from behind a souvenir stall wearing a full-length plastic apron depicting the full frontal naked torso of David. Peter said it wasn't the same as seeing the real thing.

Finally we all trooped in and stared at the one-and-a-half-storeys-high statue – 'the finest sculpture of a man in existence' according to a brochure. In truth the head is disproportionate and so is the right hand. A brochure said Michelangelo wanted to emphasise these aspects but personally I think he just got it wrong. All the same the statue is very good for a 29-year-old. The rest of the galleries were filled with a tedious variety of ecclesiastical sculptures, female busts, paintings and regalia and, as Alan observed, half seriously, 'Once you've seen one you've seen the lot.'

I now know the reason we found it all so tedious: it was Stendhal's syndrome.

The syndrome, according to Italian psychologists, specifically 'strikes culture vultures gazing at Florence's Renaissance treasures'. They seriously warn that 'trying to see too many artistic and historical artefacts in too short a time can cause dizziness, panic, paranoia and even madness'. It's called Stendhal's after the 19th century French novelist who first drew attention to the 'head-spinning disorientation some tourists experience when they encounter Florentine masterpieces'. Stendhal, late in the 1700s, almost collapsed when he saw Giotto's ceiling frescos at Santa Croce. We were indeed all reeling by the time we had seen Florence's overwhelming Duomo – even the mind-boggling ornateness of its floor was overwhelming. So was the Campanile and the incredibly ornate East Door of the Bapistry and Donatello's David and Giambologna's Mercury and Michelangelo's Bacchus and the Piazza della Signoria ...

The passer-by would have viewed the six of us with sympathy mixed, perhaps, with alarm as we slumped, thoroughly exhausted, into the chairs of a pizzeria and sank a beer. Alan then showed us on the screen of his new digital camera a truly brilliant photograph of David that he had 'sneaked'. This was quite brave of him for photography is forbidden in the museum and he could have been marched off and forced to empty all the pixels out of his camera. Alan, a quiet and modest person, was becoming what we newspapermen call 'a hardened photographer' and despite our fatigue we slowly rose to our feet and saluted him.

Back in Certaldo that evening, hot and weary, we sat at a pavement café in the main street in the lower town and, as the sun went down we watched, more or less in silence, the grand parade of seriously beautiful young women in the EU uniform of tight top, bare midriff and skin-tight jeans emerging like newly hatched butterflies. Outside the bar next door a row of old men sat ogling them.

'Look at those dirty old men ogling,' said Rex. We shook our heads and expressed hopes that we would never descend to that.

Chapter Seven

After breakfast in Certaldo we met Emily Thorp, Tuscan route manager for ATG Oxford, who introduced us to our bikes. Over her shoulder we could see, on a distant hill, our destination, San Gimignano with its 15 towers – all that is left of the 75 that existed 500 years ago. Families built them not only as refuges for when the enemy came but also to show off their wealth for there were no Ferraris in those days. In between was an undulating landscape through which we were about to cycle – a mosaic of vineyards and olive groves that predated the Romans. We had debated taking a circuitous and more challenging route to San Gimignano. We often took more challenging routes, usually by mistake. In appraising the rounded Tuscan hills we thought we could easily cycle up them and that we need dismount only for the occasional beer, wine tasting, snack, lunch, tea, historical site or interesting tree, shrub or bird or to exchange views on the weather.

Astride our new steeds we gingerly freewheeled down the very steep medieval alleyways of upper Certaldo, down through the new part of town and then across the River Elsa where the road immediately began to climb what was said to be the steepest hill of our Tuscany route. The temperature was already 30 degrees yet it was barely 8.30 am.

As leader I brought up the rear. I frequently did this, especially on hills. I often lost sight of the others for periods long enough to forget what they looked like and even their names. The two tallest, Richard and Alan, rarely dismounted even on the toughest hill yet both had legs strapped up because of rugby injuries from long ago. I made a private vow to get myself a knee guard for knee guards look very macho – even if one is wearing yellow-trimmed ankle socks. In addition Alan was recovering from 'flu and, because he had been badly spoiled as a young man (a tree rolled on him while lumber jacking in the Yukon), his vertebrae frequently conspired to remind him of their injured presence. Then there was Harvey, recovering from recent surgery, and his old colleague, Rex, still not fully re-covered from a really miserable case of shingles. There was Peter too – he was badly scarred from a fairly recent major heart opera-tion yet he was never far behind the others. I let them all go ahead, especially going up hills. It would have been churlish to have over-taken these human wrecks.

[*This is very sad stuff, particularly as it is fairly accurate. And especially because I am unable to edit it as I would wish. Nor is it possible to change the nasty phrase 'human wrecks' into something more believable, such as 'inhuman Rex'. But let me not burden you, dear reader, with the disappointments of editing an-other writer's narrative. Focus rather, on the perils and tribulations listed below. – Ed*]

We summited near the village of Pancole where we saw an ele-gant hotel set in terraced, park-like grounds with tables beneath umbrella pines and cedars. Birds sang and bougainvillea, hydran-geas and hibiscus blossomed everywhere. Fearing dehydration we stopped there and ordered a long cold beer. I am ashamed to say we sat under the trees for two hours – yet we had done only 6.6km.

Rehydration complete, we descended a long hill.

Our famous consultant, the *Tour de Italie* veteran, Alan van Heer-den, had warned us at a lunch some weeks before: 'Always wear a helmet!' Cyclists had been killed for want of a helmet, he said – and he himself would never consider cycling without one. But a really good helmet cost at least R800 and we were reluctant to buy one. At our next lunch a friend of Van Heerden, Vincent Stevens of Omnico in Randburg, presented each of us with six ultra-lightweight silver Bell helmets – the very best one can buy. It had specially designed vents for the wind to pass through. Richard claimed to be able to play tunes thought the vents by inclining his head this way and that but I think he was kidding. But would Harvey wear his helmet? (Answers on a postcard please.) Instead he wore a wide-brimmed hat. One reason was that he had had an operation on his ear lobe that had not quite healed and he had to protect it from the sun. Peter, a redhead and therefore susceptible to the sun, also had to wear a wide-brimmed hat but he fitted his helmet over the top of it so that the whole assemblage looked like a Spanish conquistador's helmet.

We gathered speed down the long hill which was moderately busy with traffic. Halfway down we found Harvey was no longer with us and we went back for him to find him on the side of the road with several bits of bark missing and, unbeknown to us at the time, two cracked ribs. He said his hat had nearly blown off and as he grabbed at it his faithful steed got a fright and threw him off. One thing about Italian drivers – they slow down when they see somebody sprawled in the road. We watched anxiously as Harvey remounted. It was, he said, essential to remount immediately after being thrown because first it shows the bike who is boss, second, if you don't you will live in fear of bikes for the rest of your life and will want to climb up a tree whenever one comes near. It was only later, when he tried to laugh and had suddenly to clutch his chest that he suspected serious damage. He soldiered on but from that day he wore his Bell helmet over his hat.

[*Corrective and helpful footnote: Because of my injured ribs I sought out in Siena a medical fellow who gave me the best pain-reliever known to man. The discovery was extremely fortunate because my hurt was invisible, and no Italian doctor would x-ray my suspected internal wounds – let alone allow me to wear a bandage like a badge around my chest, or better still, my head. Instead, I was directed to the surgery of an Italian pharmacist who turned out to be a keen cyclist. He prescribed a little bottle of medicine, which I feared would pay for most of his yacht. But he was a man of his Hippocratic oath. The bottle, costing less than an arm, carried a label showing a pretty woman rubbing her legs. That, said the pharmacist, was what it was meant for. Women used it to ease aching legs, but he'd discovered it was much better for broken ribs. So I rubbed it on my chest and thought of lovely legs – and sure enough, I instantly felt bella bella, as I think they say in Siena.*

Send money in a brown envelope, and I'll send you the name on the bottle. – Ed]

As we cycled towards San Gimignano I was ushered into the lead. I had begun to suspect that my companions liked to keep me in sight because I carried all the hotel vouchers. I recalled cycling down the Danube in 2002 and I somehow became separated from the peloton. The five waited in a beer garden and were pathetically relieved to have their leader back with them. Rex, I recall, then asked if he could see the hotel vouchers and, although it was quite unlike him, he forgot to hand them back. But thereafter they set a cracking pace and I managed to catch them up only an hour or two later and only because they had, once again, stopped at a *biergarten* and were having a rollicking party. I said how delighted I was to see them so relaxed. I was mindful of how formal they had all been early that morning when I had emerged from my room scratching my stomach with both hands and yawning only to find them standing to attention next to their machines in their resplendent livery, bicycle pumps at the slope. Although I was, technically speaking, the *obergruppenführer* I was nevertheless quite touched by this demonstration of respect. After a brief inspection I told them to stand at ease.

After five hours of blissful cycling in brilliant sunshine from Certaldo I led *Tour de Farce III* under the arch in the outer wall of San Gimignano and then up the steep narrow Via del Castello that opens on to the Piazza della Cisterna. The 'cisterna' is a central well – situated curiously right at the highest point of 'San Jimmy' – where for centuries people had gathered daily to discuss the latest hangings, burnings, religious massacres and soccer games. I couldn't help thinking that if the medieval crowd came back to life and gathered at the cisterna the only unfamiliar sight would have been us six Martians in our silver Bell helmets.

Our hotel, the Leon Bianco was on the Piazza della Cisterna from which the town's roads radiated, all dipping steeply away to the surrounding fields far below. We sat outside a café surveying the square from beneath a sun umbrella and, as the afternoon cooled, we watched the inhabitants wending their way up the hill for their evening promenade. One would think that people such as the Tuscans who live in summit towns would be fit and strong of leg like Sherpas. In fact, the more senior denizens are short and stocky and most were limping or badly bowlegged, and many used crutches and sticks. They looked for the entire world like the tail end of the Retreat from Moscow.

San Gimignano was founded by the Etruscans centuries before the Roman Empire. Frances Mayer in her book, *Under the Tuscan Sun*, neatly describes such places as 'thousands of years deep'. The town is named after an obscure saint who, when its walls were besieged by the Goths in 550, came down from the clouds in golden armour and beat them off. One wonders what people smoked in those days.

Round the corner from our hotel was the broad Piazza del Duomo which is something of an amphitheatre and here we sat on some church steps and listened to an orchestra playing in a cavernous Romanesque alcove – no tickets needed. One simply found a place to sit and enjoy classical and popular orchestral music. Afterwards, from this square, Richard and I climbed 'San Jimmy's' tallest tower, the 60-metres-high, 700-year-old stone-built Torre Grossa. We were rewarded by a 360-degree view of Tuscany's soft hills, geometrically patterned with stripes (the neat rows of vines), blobs (the blue-grey trees in the olive groves) and decorated by isolated rows of vertical cypresses like black candles – many planted in memory of locals who died in latter-day wars.

A newspaper colleague in South Africa told me there's some bomb damage not far from San Gimignano caused by his brother who was a Spitfire pilot in World War II. The pilot found himself in a situation where he had to jettison two bombs suspended beneath his wings. In trying to avoid hitting a village he miscalculated and, to his dismay, demolished a centuries-old building on the edge of the village and made a deep hole in an orchard. Years later the pilot, who now lives in Umbria, visited the village and asked the locals to show him where the two bombs landed. The locals, without knowing he was the pilot, eagerly showed him the ruin and, a distance beyond it, the still-visible crater where the second bomb landed. They shook their heads at the memory of that infamous 'raid' and then an elder spat out the Italian equivalent of, 'Bloody Australians!' The former pilot shook his head in sympathy.

Harvey and Rex visited the Museo della Tortura next to our hotel and emerged a trifle pale from the experience. One of the diabolical instruments they described was a heavy iron collar with spikes on the inside. It was clamped around the victim's neck so that he had difficulty swallowing. Whatever movement he made, one or two spikes would dig in. Unable to lie down, he was free to wander around until, after a month or so, septicaemia mercifully killed him. Some instruments were even more horrific and were used by religious Gauleiters to punish people. [*The only modern instrument of torture that comes near these apparatuses, or apparati, as old-fashioned editors say, is the bicycle saddle. – Ed*]

Next day we were cycling in tight formation along a *strada bianca* (literally a 'white road' – an unsurfaced but smooth gravel farm road) when Rex, who sometimes had to share a room with Harvey, announced that Harvey talked in his sleep. Naturally we were all agog.

'What about?' we asked.

'I don't know,' said Rex. 'It's so boring I fall asleep again.'

[*This is a sad case that demonstrates how snorers deny their own snoring and falsely accuse others. In truth, I was not asleep – could not sleep – and was simply trying to tell Rex to reduce his own volume. – Ed*]

One loses a litre an hour cycling in hot weather. A litre of water weighs 1kg. Having forgotten to fill my water bottle I worked out that as we had five hours to go to our next night stop, Monteriggioni, I'd be 5kg lighter – assuming we did not stop. It was not to be. At the crest of a long hill, we found a gaggle of comparatively nearly new buildings – say 16th century – but nowhere that sold refreshments. Some of my companions were beginning to grizzle when Rex saw a sign reading 'Coop'. Behind the sign was a shop with refrigerators and other non-medieval marvels. An agricultural co-op! Peter and I walked in. We were dressed in our dazzling cycling gear and streamlined helmets and the customers froze in whatever positions they happened to be in and followed us with their eyes. One woman, who was bending down at the time, peered at us from under her armpit. The shopkeeper, a kindly woman, ignoring three or four locals who were queuing to pay her, said to us, '*Nel gabinetto non c'e carta igienica,'* or something like that. I think it's Italian for, 'What-a can I do for-a you?' Peter, who had picked up a surprising amount of Italian asked if we could get ham and tomato rolls and six bottles of cold *birra* but he insisted she serve her other customers first. She made a brief statement to the hill tribe who all made sympathetic cries like, *'Chiami un vigile!'* I think this means, 'For San Petro's sake feed these giant mutant insects first and get them out of here.'

We were ushered to an outside table and served six huge bottles of beer – we never saw larger – and 15 minutes later came six Nobel Prize-winning ham rolls. The customers whom we had kept waiting were unfazed and cheerfully waved to us as they left. Italians are like that – kind and patient. Only when they become officials do they turn into Mussolinis.

One of the attractions of cycling in autumn is that one can stop and pick figs and blackberries along the roadside. I had never seen such perfect figs – not one had been stung or pecked and all had been grown for the wayfarer.

As we neared the hill on which was perched the dramatic citadel of Monteriggioni I once again led the peloton across the intervening valley – a valley that had seen many historical figures leading their armies – Hannibal and Charlemagne and, more recently, the landscape had been churned by German Panzers and Allied tanks. Passing through a narrow entrance in the wall we entered the tiny, totally contained, circular town of Monteriggioni. It is a three-street fortress surrounded by an ancient turreted wall just over 500m around. The town of 65 people gets quite a few morose lines in Dante's *Inferno* probably because, I think, the poet was as shocked as we were by the restaurant prices. But the food was outstanding and people come from over the hills and far away to eat there. Our rooms had a breathtaking view towards distant hills punctuated with tall cypresses. It was all so peaceful that it was hard to comprehend how often in the past the smoke of war has drifted across it.

Once we'd settled down Harvey began reading aloud from some brochures he'd picked up describing the region. The writing might have sounded fine in Italian but in translation it made a powerful emetic. 'Close your eyes,' said Harvey, 'think of a 15th century work by Fra Filippo Lipi and listen to this description of where we are:

'[She] is ... the nymph of the Chianti, the soul of this land. Brambles and grapevines make up her hair, the wind is her breath, sparkling streams reflect her eyes, wine flows in her veins, and rolling hills are the contours of her body. Her smile shines like the sun, and she is as proud as a castle and gentle as an abbey. She is simultaneously earthy and ascetic, older than time while elegant in her youthfulness. She is endowed with mysterious magic and loves to be on display, to express herself to welcome visitors and be an object of desire ...

'And to think,' said Harvey, 'we rode all over her!'

Next day we cycled to one of the best preserved medieval cities in the world, Siena, Dante's 'antechamber to Paradise'. Like all great cities Siena is filled with surprises and one is reminded of Ancient Rome's sensible ban on naked concrete and its dictum that there must always be detail to excite the eye. We arrived in Siena at noon and at our central and very pleasant B&B – the Piccolo Hotel Etruria. We quickly changed and began to explore the narrow shaded streets. We passed through a dark arcade and were startled to find ourselves suddenly gazing across the dazzling Piazza del Campo, a vast sunny space dominated by one of the world's most famous towers – the soaring Torre de Mangia. This is where the frenzied annual bareback horse race, di Palio, takes place and where non-conformists were once burned at the stake.

Harvey (I discovered only months later) was seriously worried about his chest pains and in Siena was even contemplating having to fly home. He disappeared in the square trying to find a doctor but the best he could do was a chemist who nevertheless gave him a thorough examination and diagnosed two cracked ribs. The chemist said nothing could be done apart from taking painkillers and giving up laughing for at least two weeks.

We visited Siena's spectacular Cathedral whose detail left our senses reeling. We climbed to a lookout high above the Unfinished Nave – unfinished because the 14th century Black Plague wiped out a third of Siena's people and there were simply not enough builders and masons to carry on. From here we had a breathtaking view over the whole of Siena, its pink buildings glowing in the late afternoon light. Church bells rang from literally all around us and, from below in the tangled web of streets, a drummer beat an incessant but expert tattoo. Italians love parading in medieval costume, beating drums and waving large flags.

We had a three-day hiatus after Siena before doing the week-long Umbria ride and the Tuscan tourist authority arranged for us to explore Lower Tuscany by car – in fact Avis kindly provided us with two cars. We wanted to see the Leaning Tower of Pisa before the whole lot came down. Using the new autostrada we drove through the region in which we had just spent a week cycling and, as we recognised distant hills over which we had previously toiled, we were filled with admiration of ourselves. Avis, whom I had often used before in Europe, had allocated us two Fiats designed for sawn-off Italians but they proved perfectly adequate for the six of us. It was the luggage that had us beat – at least until a Sienese clerk with a doctorate in packing car boots demonstrated how to stow luggage economically in ten seconds.

Once in Pisa I was quite startled by the angle of the Leaning Tower. I recalled seeing its rival – the leaning tower in Belfast, Ireland, a couple of years before. Belfast's central clock tower leans every bit as alarmingly. Belfast playwright, Ken McElroy, told me, 'It's better than the Leaning Tower of Pisa. It not only has the inclination – it also has the time.'

I was surprised to see that ALL the medieval buildings in Pisa's Campo dei Miracoli were leaning – and in every which way. I said we ought to mention this to the authorities but my colleagues said they had probably noticed. In 1994 engineers dug 50 metres down to bedrock beneath the overhanging 14 000-ton tower when it gave an audible groan before suddenly showering dust upon them and tilting a few more millimetres. This must have loosened some bowels. Today the Leaning Tower of Pisa is anchored to the bedrock and has righted itself by 400 mm. We could have climbed to the top of the 900-year-old tower but it meant a two-hour wait so we settled instead for a pizza in a pizzeria in a piazza next to a Pisa palazzo. Then we set off to return to Lower Tuscany.

We were booked into the inexpensive but quite grand Hotel Palazzuolo in San Quirico d'Orcia whose aristocratic owner, Leonardo Simonelli-Santi, had organised a wine tasting for us. Alas, we arrived two hours late, having twice become hopelessly lost. The person we entrusted to telephone our host to say we'd be late did not get through. But the noble vintner, who was leaving for the United Kingdom that evening, brushed aside our apologies and led us to his ancient winery. Leonardo owns some delightful corners of this 8th century town and, we unanimously agreed, produces some very fine red wine named Orcia after the name of the valley. He also produces export olive oil and loves showing visitors around both his winery and olivery. Although I can certainly tell extra-virgin olive oil from, say, Caltex, I found I was not much good at judging one olive oil against another but Peter, who has some cullinary skills and recalled the excellent olive oil he tasted when dining with Margaret Thatcher at Chequers, was convincing in his unstinting approval of the oil we tasted. Some of it was from trees planted by the Simonelli-Santi family almost 500 years ago.

San Quirico is named after Saint Quiricus, a five-year-old boy slain by Romans because he said he was a Christian. Slaughtering people has, over the centuries, been a popular pastime in Umbria and must have kept a lot of people out of mischief.

We noticed that now we had cars we tended to try to see too much, and we certainly missed out on the aromas and sounds of the countryside. It was a bit like riffling through a book, looking only at the pictures. Nevertheless the fast pace served our purpose and we were able to savour the ancient places where cyclists stay over – such as Pienza. This is a small medieval city with a balcony view of Lower Tuscany. The guidebook says it has a population of '2 500 souls' which made it sound like a ship about to hit an iceberg. Oddly enough, it is perched on an unstable, wave-like contour and, as a result, ominous cracks have appeared in Pienza's cathedral. The basilica's slow disintegration is partly because of a 1462 Papal decree that structurally it must never be touched.

We savoured Pienza's warm stonework and hanging baskets of vivid geraniums and were sorry not to have had more time there but we'd had to park our cars illegally and were anxious to avoid trouble with the police. That is until we got to Montelcino where we sat at a corner café and watched two incredibly beautiful and well-designed young policewomen patrolling up and down on high heels and we mused how difficult it would be for them to run after a miscreant. Rex said they wouldn't have to – offenders would gladly surrender.

Wherever one looks in Tuscany there are religious structures, some dating back to the earliest Christian era. Stone floors have been polished smooth by the feet of the devout and the curious. The soaring, dark interiors are lit only by shafts of sunlight coming through stained-glass windows and we were often overawed by the antiquity and the incredible skills and devotion of the ancient civil engineers, masons, architects and artists.

We went on to Grosetto on the coastal plain and paid around R100 each to visit the Maremma National Park whose main excitement seemed to be its amiable horses and cows. The popular, long narrow beach is, to give it its full credit, perfectly horrible and is fringed by the collapsed wreckage of a long-dead forest. We wondered what had killed the trees. It was like a scene from Neville Shute's nuclear war novel, *On the Beach*. I was amazed by the numbers of sunbathers reclining along this singularly unattractive narrow strip of Tyrrhenian coast.

There was a magnificent notice comprising a few thousand words in Italian, German, French and English, listing all the things you were not allowed to do. They were mostly incomprehensible, one of them reading:

> *To occupy with deckchairs, beach ombrellas, tools, sheets and so on; also nauticals unities except rescue unities, 5 mtrs far away from the sea shore left to the free transit and forbidden to stand on.*

We drove south to what seems to be a nameless Capri-like island, technically, I suppose, a peninsula because it was accessible by causeway. Beneath the waves one can see the Etruscan foundations of its once thriving port, Ortobello. We had time only to motor around the palm-fringed peninsula and gawk briefly at the luxurious yachts at Porto Santo Stefano.

Touring by car one really does get no more than an impression of a country and we were quite relieved to get back to our bed-and-breakfast accommodation 10km inland on the edge of the city of Grosetto. It was in a large stone farmhouse called the Razza del Casalone whose cheerful hostess was entertaining a score of cerebral palsied youngsters holidaying there, at her expense, in a specially-built annex. We were greatly touched by her lively and happy rapport with them although none could speak coherently. The elaborate breakfast was the best we had in Italy – possibly the best we'd had anywhere.

We rounded off our exploration of Lower Tuscany in a little town straight out of a film set, Campagnatico, which was having its annual round-the-houses donkey race. Whether it was intended as a parody of Siena's Palio I don't know but it was clearly a very serious race. I noticed one donkey was named Bicchi. We drove round and round seeking Villa Bellaria, our B&B for the night and kept finding ourselves back at the imposing iron gates of a grand walled villa. Then we realised this was it – this was Villa Bellaria. It was an archetypal Roman villa with a vast terraced garden and mossy statues as well as a large, incongruous, bright blue swimming pool below the ancient orchard. Our elegant hostess, Luisa Querci della Rovere, who owned many local farms, invited us to dine in the main house. We were so impressed by the old-world charm of the place that we went down for dinner wearing jackets and ties. Luisa's family, in shorts and t-shirts, clearly thought us quaint.

Into Umbria

By now we realised there was no time to intelligently pioneer a cycle route clean across Italy. Like our abortive mission to find the source of the Danube we conveniently never again mentioned our quest for a trans-Italian route. I believe such a route is possible and that it would be internationally attractive but one would need a few weeks to reconnoitre it and a great deal more help from the central tourist authority than one would be likely to get. Instead we drove to Perugia where we dropped the cars off at Avis and went to the main railway station to get a train to Todi 40km away. There we would pick up our next set of bikes for the second stage of *Tour de Farce III* and pedal north through Umbria to Assisi.

At Perugia station we encountered once more the indifference of Italian officials which is sometimes on a par with the old communist countries where there was no incentive for officials to be helpful because the state could neither fire them for ineptitude nor reward them for initiative. To make things worse it was Sunday and Italians tend to go into neutral on Sundays. We asked the lethargic ticket clerk for six tickets to Todi. He said, 'No trains.' We couldn't believe it. We asked at three different places. 'No trains,' they insisted. An official said we should try next morning. I phoned our hotel in Todi to ask how people got there from Perugia on a Sunday afternoon and he said, 'There are plenty of trains.' I informed the ticket office of this but they were adamant: 'No trains!' Then a stranger walked over and told us that a few hundred metres along the road was another station with a regular service to Todi. We got there just in time to catch the 2 pm train. The service was run by private enterprise and Italian officials, beholden to the government and its rather comical quasi-communist attitude, are not prepared to inform people about enterprises run by private enterprise.

The Roman town of Todi is, like so many of Italy's medieval towns, built on a hill – a particularly steep hill. Fortunately, as the train drew in a bus drew up and we were driven to the summit and heaped outside the Hotel Fonte Cesia with our luggage. The hotel was on the large main square and we arrived just in time to see traders in the square packing up their stalls after a Sunday market specialising in antiques and interesting old junk. The square affords an elevated view of the rolling hills of Umbria and the valley carved by the Tiber.

Next morning our bikes were delivered to the hotel's pool deck where a group of athletic young American cyclists with serious racing bikes asked Rex and Harvey where we were heading. They had to confess they had no idea. The Americans looked at them in silence for a long time. If they'd asked any of us we would have answered similarly because our destination had a rather forgettable name – Giano dell'Umbria.

All we knew was that for the next few days we would be cycling in roughly a northerly direction and we were yet to familiarise ourselves with the region's scattered towns and villages. Anyway, we had a more pressing question facing us – how to find our way out of the hotel whose geography was exceedingly complicated. It became pure comedy but, once dignity had been restored and, resplendent in our white cycling togs, we found our way on to the piazza where I led the peloton slowly across the square southwards and halfway down an incredibly steep hill. Richard loudly questioned my direction. He was right. We should have headed in the opposite direction. We now had to push our bikes back up the hill and once more afford the locals some quiet entertainment as we traced our route back across the square.

Todi, sitting like a stone crown on a high hilltop, remained in sight for a long time. It seemed to be always there like a toffee paper sticking to one's shoe. We cruised along a winding valley through olive groves and past stone farmhouses. Lunchtime came without sighting anywhere to buy refreshments. Then we struck a long, long hill that climbed through a forest with gaps that afforded some magnificent vistas. It was hot. Very hot. We rested under some trees and drank the last of our water. At 2.00 pm, after more than five hours' cycling, we came across a large hillside inn where we fell upon a mug of beer and then a large sandwich and then another beer for we were badly dehydrated. And then, as we reluctantly remounted to continue up the mountain expecting, for some reason, another 5km of uphill, Rex read aloud the name of the hotel – Hotel Park Montecerreto. I hauled out our itinerary and there it was – we were booked into the Hotel Park Montecerreto. The staff was highly amused by all the forehead slapping that followed our discovery. What confused us was that there was no sign at all of the village of Giano dell'Umbria. We found it that evening when we strolled 500 metres down the hill, took a right turn along a narrow country lane and there, hidden behind the hill, was this fortified Roman rabbit warren of a village whose stone houses seemed to clutch at each other. Narrow cobbled alleyways burrowed among them. We detected no sign of life except for the sound of television or radio programmes coming from behind closed shutters. We went inside the dark and ancient Church of San Francesco whose frescoes date back to the Middle Ages. It was 7.00 pm and still half an hour before the restaurant opened and the sun had much warmth left in it. We found some chairs and a table in the otherwise empty Piazza Municipale and from its tiny single shop, whose interior was as dark as San Francesco's, we bought Campari and soda and relaxed in the square.

The restaurant about which we had been tipped off was the Ristorante Il Buongustaio and was entered through what looked like an accidental gap in a ruined stone wall. The restaurant's interior was so archetypal Umbrian and so atmospheric it could have been one of those meticulously contrived Italian *ristorantes* one finds in London or New York or Gauteng – except this was real, this was genuine, and when one stepped outside there would be no Hackney cabs, no yellow taxis, no skyscrapers and urban noises and smells – just ancient aromatic Umbria and the sound of crickets. The generous antipasto was followed by an unforgettable multi-course meal that, with wine and grappa, cost us so little we felt guilty.

Next day, after freewheeling down the hill and past Giano dell'Umbria and then for several blessed minutes steeply down into the Tiber valley we decided to buy food for a picnic lunch. We had always said we should picnic more but had never yet succeeded in organising ourselves. On the rare occasions we did eat alfresco it was usually sitting on some stone steps in a drafty corner of a bleak village square.

Late in the morning we stopped at a village and bought baguettes, butter, meat slices, cheeses, olives, beer and water before cycling on. We pedalled along farm roads in the flat, almost treeless floodplain but we saw no shady spots for picnicking and we began to worry about the beer getting warm and the butter melting. On we pedalled. The heat was intense and our thirst became genuine. In desperation we decided to picnic in the roadside grass beside a *strada bianca*. A few oaks provided shade. We set about the food and drank all the beer and, one by one, hats over our faces, we fell asleep next to our bikes. The scene, sneakily photographed by our hardened photographer, resembled a horror roadside accident with scattered bodies and bikes.

The day's ride ended with a gentle 3km climb up to the walled 14th century town of Montefalco – the Ringhiera dell'Umbria (Balcony of Umbria). We arrived feeling peckish and ordered a pizza for lunch not realising it would be the size of a cartwheel. It was helped down by an exceptional Chianti. It was again all incredibly cheap. Throughout that night a thunderstorm distantly rumbled and flickered. Twice I was awakened by thunder but the next day, after a brief shower, dawned bright and sunny. Harvey and I ambled up to an ATM in the town square after breakfast, both of us needing to cash some money. Incongruously the brand-new machine was set into a medieval stone wall. Its complicated keyboard was new to our experience and had us baffled.

[*The writer, in one of his columns, gave the impression that he and I had practically blown up the bank in Montefalco and I cannot miss this opportunity to give some background to this event. First, it should be known that we were innocent. We were innocent Luddite pastoralists trying to survive in a world of wicked machinery. So it was with a caution bordering on paranoia that we approached the new-fangled Autobank machine set in a 13th century stone wall in one of the town's cobbled squares. We knew that these latest machines calculate the exchange rate of euros, dollars, pounds, rands or rupees and then spit bank notes at you at a speed that does not allow you to catch your breath. James, standing well back, had tentatively stabbed at some of the keys.*

'Don't let go of your credit card until that machine promises to give you money,' I warned him.

Nothing happened.

Noticing a second, minor pad of keys, I stepped into the breach. I cautiously touched one of the smaller buttons with the tip of my left index finger. BOINNGGG! The noise was deafening. The wall – the whole square – shuddered and our teeth rattled. We jumped to a height that would have won gold at the Olympics. While putting our shoes back on, we realised we were standing below a bell tower. The two-ton bell must have been triggered, we figured, by some evil force when I touched the Autobank button. It struck only once.

We asked not for whom the bell tolled. Instead we hurriedly returned to the hotel, collected our bikes and rode out of town. – Ed]

I have long had a problem with cash cards. Useful though they are I have a recurring nightmare that one day some 12-year-old hacker will ferret out my PIN and clean me out. I was unimpressed when, a couple of years ago, I received a letter that began, 'Dear Valued Cardholder' and which was accompanied by an unsolicited credit card and a detailed explanation about how I could pound even greater cascades of money from almost any type of machine including automatic dishwashers. The very sight of this card, it intimated, would cause international hotels and branches of Gucci to slobber over my size nines, begging to be of service. I placed the card among the others in my card album which I carry strapped to my person. After all, we Dear Valued Cardholders, have a bounden duty to ensure that these cards do not fall into the Wrong Hands. There's enough buying power in these cards to bring down the national economy. An unscrupulous person could, by playing one card account against another, screw up a nation's banking system as if it were an empty chip packet.

Automatic bank machines have minds of their own and are inclined to intimidate the nervous. They may well flash an illuminated bright green message that attracts moths from ten kilometres away reading, WE HAVE A PROBLEM. What it really means is YOU have a problem. Try telling it that you are a DVC and it will be unimpressed; try thumping it and you get a change of message to FESTIVE GREETINGS TO ALL OUR CARDHOLDERS! or CARD RETAINED – SEE MANAGER.

I once wrote to my bank:

Dear Valued Card Dealer

In the good old days, before I became just another overspending DVC I would go to the bank, offer a cheque, and a smiling young lady named Zelda would greet me by name and thrust cash upon me. When you use real folding money there are certain healthy restraints but using plastic money is like using casino chips – it does not feel like real money. You lose touch with reality, especially in hardware shops and at the delicatessen counter.

I lie abed tortured at night by thoughts of what might happen if my card fell into the Wrong Hands, like my wife's. I have, as a result, become irritable and find myself shouting at strangers and damaging property. My doctor diagnoses cardio-rascibility and I may be forced to sue.

Yours truly – 174-494-087

The bank never replied.

The storm had not gone away. As we cycled down the long hill from Montefalco we saw a huge blue-grey gravid cloud hanging low over the valley. We reached the point where we were to have turned off but, at that moment, the cloud, which obviously had been waiting for us, said, 'NOW!' and dumped its contents upon our heads. It was the first time, on any of our rides, that the *Tour de Farce* had encountered serious rain. As if to make up for this omission the storm lashed us with quite unnecessary enthusiasm and for an hour we huddled under a half-finished building, shivering and wet through. Being of stout heart we unanimously agreed to chicken out of the prescribed 50 or 60km route to Bevagna and, instead, take a short cut. As we entered its portals the rain stopped and the sun beamed down as if the whole thing had been a practical joke.

We unanimously resolved to cycle again that afternoon to make up for having missed the longer ride and perhaps witness at least some of the proper route. We had a pre-lunch beer. And remembering what Peter's doctor had told him about beer being the best beverage after a hot day's cycling, we had a second. *[One would be foolish to ignore medical advice considering how much it costs. – Ed]* This was followed by a long lunch with wine after which we were overcome by an overpowering lethargy – obviously nature's warning that our frenetic race to Bevagna had taken far more out of us than we had realised. So, with the exception of Richard who cycled another 30km to Spello and back, we went to our hotel, the Palazzo Brunamonte, and had a siesta and then read a little before striking out on foot to explore the 2 000-year-old town.

We sat for a time in the beautifully preserved medieval Piazza Silvestri. (The reader may be confused with all these pizzas and piazzas. It is important to know that a piazza is as different from a pizza as a steel mill is different from a lettuce. A plaza is also quite different. For a start a plaza has only one z – I think.) At precisely 8.00 pm the big clock in the piazza struck 13. No kidding. Then a distant clock struck 3 followed by another that struck 7. At six next morning the big clock struck 13 again. Salvador Dali would have loved this place.

Religious experience

After one has toured Tuscany and Umbria one town or even city tends to merge with the next in one's memory, but Assisi was in a class of its own. One can never forget Assisi. This is where our Umbrian ride was to end. The ride that day was the longest and coldest of our tour but it was enjoyable. We began late in the morning and after climbing 600 metres within the first 5km we came across a 15th century village, Collepino. Its interlocked stone houses were in a tight embrace. Like soccer players after scoring a goal they seemed to be trying to climb on top of one another.

Even though it was 10.30 am the village square was silent as the grave. We found a locked-up café with metal chairs and tables outside so we sat and rested. From a window high above our heads a 15th century woman shouted something like, '*Ho lasciato gli occhiali nella toeletta!*' which I think is Italian for 'Half a mo'. The problem with Italians is that they have a different word for just about everything. In no time she served us coffee, enabling us to continue up the mountain, occasionally stopping to pick wild figs. From the top we had our first view of distant Assisi, its pink stone buildings smothering a hill; we could make out domes and towers and, on the high crest above the city, a castle cocooned in scaffolding. We later learned the castle had been severely damaged in the 1997 earthquake.

We blissfully freewheeled for kilometres and then joined a major but not too busy highway following a river. Being Expedition Leader I then led the peloton as it made its historic entry through Assisi's Porta Perlici. At the end of such a ride professional cyclists would have punched the air in triumph but we had nothing against the air and in any event we would have all crashed into each other.

One can understand why Italians are indifferent to tourists when you see in places such as Assisi the cattle-like, wall-to-wall herds of visitors endlessly moving with shuffling gait and bovine apathy, following shouting tour leaders who carry little flags on long sticks so that stragglers can spot them above the crowd. It's like a slow-motion replay of the 5th century invasion of this region by the Barbarian hordes. But these latter-day invaders are armed with weapons far more messy than swords and cudgels – they are carrying sticky melting ice-cream cones.

We cycled up the long hill to the main square – the Piazza del Comune – and saw the colonnaded façade of the 2 000-year-old Roman Temple of Minerva whose interior was turned into a church in 1539 and was 'baroqued' a century later. We cautiously free-wheeled down the other side of the city, carefully picking our way through the narrow streets with their milling tourists until we descended a long, steep cobbled road and exited through the south-east *porta*. Like so many of Italy's historical cities Assisi is in an interestingly jumbled pile – there is no cheapskate piece of modern architecture in the middle to interrupt the medieval integrity; there is no conurbation beyond its walls. Beyond the walls of Assisi is a narrow fringe of low-rise buildings set among gardens with pine and cypress trees – nothing to insult the eye – and they melt into the fields, farms and orchards below. We zigzagged down and down for almost a kilometre to our interesting farmhouse hotel with an English name – Country House Hotel – a large, rambling place with a terraced garden and sizeable swimming pool.

We had become used to paying a modest surcharge for separate rooms [*Most of the team were prepared, by this time, to pay almost anything for a separate room. – Ed*] and in my case it was a huge corner room on the second floor with large windows on two sides giving a 180-degree panoramic view of central Italy.

Next morning we walked back up the steep two kilometres to the impressive Basilica of St Francis. We entered the dimly lit Upper Church with its fresco of 28 panels painted by Giotto – an almost life-size picture story of the life of the world's favourite saint. The paintings had been skilfully repaired after the 1997 earthquake had brought down part of the ceiling killing four people. Giotto's paintings were a sensation in the 14th century for they depicted real people against real scenery. The church dictatorship in those days frowned upon realism. Every few minutes a sepulchral recorded voice intoned over the public address system, 'Shhhhhh! Silence! Silento!' We shuffled past the tomb of St Francis along with bubbly nuns from Africa, awed Latino nuns and brown-robed Franciscan friars – pilgrims all. I suppose we were also pilgrims in a way.

There is no doubt that St Francis, who was a rebellious youngster often at loggerheads with his wealthy dad and who briefly fought in the cavalry (religious wars were as fashionable then as they are today), deserves the adulation he continues to receive 800 years later as Italy's patron saint. Francis forsook the wealth that could have been his and, in an era when the Church itself was pathological, committing torture and massacres, St Francis preached a reverence for life – even for human life, which was novel. He saw man as part of nature and not as its master, and he looked upon nature with a mixture of love and wonder and certainly reverence. But neither Italy nor the Church, nor almost anyone else ever learned. On our last day in Umbria – a Sunday – I was awakened at sunrise by the pealing of Assisi's church bells and, from the fields, the competing artillery of the insatiable Italian hunters. Clang! Bang! Clang! Bang! Clang! Bang!

> *All things bright and beautiful*
> *All creatures great and small;*
> *All things wise and wonderful*
> *Italians shoot them all.*

And the church continues to condone the view that man has 'dominion over every living thing' and so, as Lynn White Jr wrote in *Science* in March 1967, Christians continue to exploit nature in a mood of indifference.

We walked endlessly through the narrow medieval streets of Assisi lined with little shops crammed with religious kitsch. I was reminded of a jeweller's story about a young woman who walked into his shop and asked for a gold crucifix and was shown a plain one. 'No,' she said, 'I want one with a little man on it.' There were a million crucifixes; a million St Francises inside a million glass balls that create snow scenes when shaken; a million wooden Virgin Marys and ceramic Virgin Marys and metal and plastic ones. I wouldn't have been too surprised to see iced-lolly ones.

A million Christs on a million crosses, *il gelato* and *bier*.

Chapter Eight

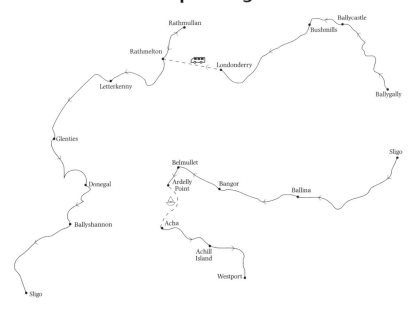

In Ireland, even if you have to cycle up endless hills against rain and wind – as we did during *Tour de Farce IV* – most destinations and the people one meets are worth the journey. What better on a wet day than a snug pub, instant good company, pleasant folk music and wit flying about like cake at a toddler's first birthday party? The Irish are so spontaneously friendly and curious about visitors that within minutes you feel you've known them all your life. There aren't many strangers in Ireland.

A few years ago I was in the basement of the Abbey Tavern in the little fishing harbour of Howth in northern Dublin, listening to an Irish ensemble, when I felt a tickle in the ribs and turned to see a

IRELAND

INSET TOP: A wet start to Tour de Farce IV at Ballygally, Northern Ireland. TOP: Giant's Causeway. CENTRE LEFT: The rope bridge at Carrick-a-Rede. LEFT: Bridge at Rathmelton where pharmacist, Tom Murray opened his chemist shop on a Sunday to tend to an injury. INSET: On a headland within sight of Scotland. Ireland is nearer to Scotland than are the Hebrides.

TOP: Barrels of Guinness arrived as we reached this pub. Coincidence?
TOP RIGHT: Richard with that 'Guinness is good for you' look; Rex – similarly content. ABOVE: The team in their Guinness livery (Harvey lost his cap within an hour). LEFT: Richard: 'But I only ordered a small Coke.' Barmaid: 'Tell me about it?'

Tour de Farce IV – Ireland

Peter maintained there are
3 107 987 pubs in Ireland but
we think he was making
the figure up. We visited
only 1 387 766 of them.

Tour de Farce IV – Ireland

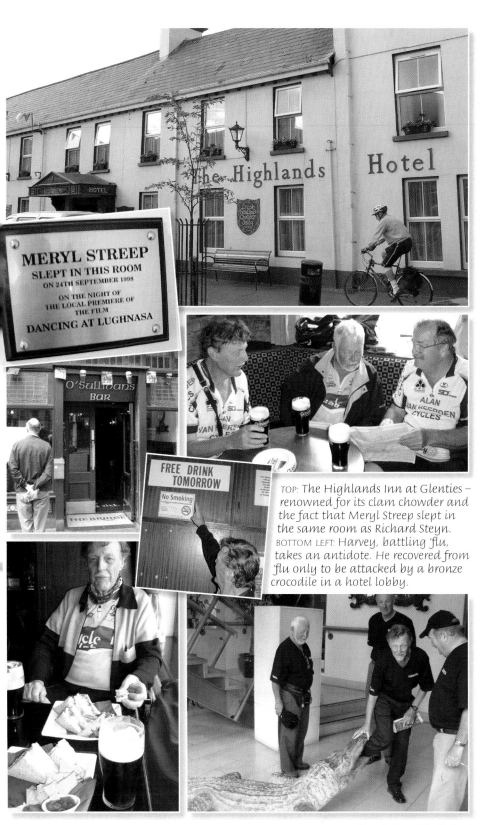

MERYL STREEP
SLEEP IN THIS ROOM
ON 24TH SEPTEMBER 1998

ON THE NIGHT OF
THE LOCAL PREMIERE OF
THE FILM
DANCING AT LUGHNASA

O'Sullivans
Bar

FREE DRINK
TOMORROW
No Smoking

TOP: The Highlands Inn at Glenties – renowned for its clam chowder and the fact that Meryl Streep slept in the same room as Richard Steyn.
BOTTOM LEFT: Harvey, battling 'flu, takes an antidote. He recovered from 'flu only to be attacked by a bronze crocodile in a hotel lobby.

Tour de Farce IV – Ireland

TOP: Day four in Londonderry began without promise. It became so wet en route to Derry that we decided to cut across country. BELOW: Rex, not trusting the Leader's advice, refers to a map. On day five the Irish blessing, 'May the road rise up to meet you', did just that and I incurred a knee injury but I bravely carried on. Somebody said I showed grit. It was embedded in my left knee.

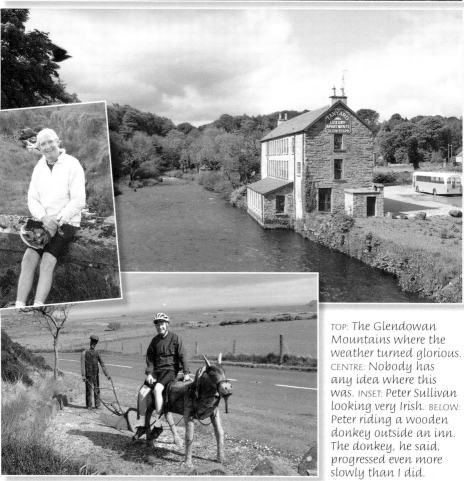

TOP: The Glendowan Mountains where the weather turned glorious. CENTRE: Nobody has any idea where this was. INSET: Peter Sullivan looking very Irish. BELOW: Peter riding a wooden donkey outside an inn. The donkey, he said, progressed even more slowly than I did.

Tour de Farce IV – Ireland

TOP: Ireland has 4 657 shades of green according to Peter. Here are 37 of them.
LEFT: Me, in civvies (having retired hurt), surrounded by admirers before we all took a hellish boat ride across Black Sod Bay.
BELOW: Farewell at Dublin airport before departing in three different directions.

Tour de Farce IV – Ireland

50s-something woman behind me and a very attractive red-headed girl behind her, smiling. I thought the action must have been accidental so simply smiled back. A couple of minutes later another tickle and I realised it was from the younger woman. She introduced herself and then her mother (who was the woman directly behind me) and then her father, a retired Irish soccer international and we spent the rest of the evening chatting away.

Even the Irish sheep dogs are friendly. One year I drove to the Isle of Innisfree – which Yeats made so famous – down the narrowest tarred road I'd ever seen. Having parked in a tiny car park I was met by an exceptionally friendly Border collie who gave me a look that said, 'Follow me!' And he led me, so help me, down through the heather to the side of the silent lough where he and I sat and gazed at the tiny, densely wooded isle. I recalled out loud as much as I could of those famous lines:

> I will arise and go now, and go to Innisfree,
> And a small cabin build there, of clay and wattle made:
> Nine bean rows will I have there, a hive for the honeybee,
> And live alone in a bee-loud glade.

You can do that sort of thing in Ireland – talk to animals. The dog, I could see, knew the lines by heart. I asked him how on earth Yeats could have built a cabin on such a tiny island AND still find room for nine rows of beans. The dog looked up and laughed silently in that way collies have.

Despite their unhappy history – or, maybe, because of it – the Irish have adopted a quick and unique sense of humour – dry and rarely at anybody's expense. During our tour Richard pointed to a sign in an inn in County Sligo announcing: FREE DRINKS TOMORROW. Another read: 'The Management will not be responsible for any injuries incurred in the mad rush for the door at closing time.'

It would be disingenuous of me not to mention at the outset that things had changed since the first three tours. We discovered that Richard had broken the rules; he had begun to take cycling seriously. The first sign was when he admitted, very quietly – just as a man might confess to having a secret passion for collecting pictures of Hillary Clinton – that he had recently taken part in a cycle road race. The writing is on the wall, we said to each other as soon as he was out of earshot. He was already a very strong cyclist who could double or treble what I could do in a given time. 'We are going to be cycling with a Lance Armstrong,' somebody said. Next he was cycling on Sunday mornings in the Suikerboschrand, a range of mountains 30km south of Johannesburg and noted for its notoriously long hills. Then he entered the 94.7 race organised by Radio 94.7. This is a formidable Johannesburg road race of 100km held in the heat of summer. He told us he finished in '3 hours and 90 minutes'. Next he had entered the world's biggest cycle race – the Argus, a notoriously tough race through the mountains of the Cape Peninsula. Both these events – the Argus and the 94.7 – call for the closing off of important arterial roads sometimes resulting in road rage as angry motorists have to make long detours. These races attract some of the top people in commerce and industry, some riding bikes costing as much as a Harley Davidson and wearing gaudy *haute couture* apparel. It was simply not seemly for a member of the *Tour de Farce* to be seen hobnobbing with such people. We were, as Richard had himself observed, into coarse cycling, not the drop-handlebar stuff. We were slightly mollified when I circulated an article that suggested long-distance cycle races are probably doomed. The Chronosplit system will put an end to them.

The present-day system uses a mat which contestants have to cycle over and it records their time and race number. According to Gus Ferguson – he is a long-distance cyclist as well as a noted writer of comic verse as well as a cartoonist and pharmacist in Plumstead in the Cape – the Chronosplit system is being upgraded. Writing in the pharmacists' newsletter, *Tincture Press,* he said that apart from being able to scan the name, age, sex and seeded category of each contestant, new advanced diagnostic software now allows the system to 'read critical data' that includes the health and wellbeing of athletes as they pass. A pilot study using 11 000 cyclists had already diagnosed in competitors, as they passed over a special mat at the start, hypertension, clinical depression, diabetes, low sperm count and athlete's foot, and accurately determined IQ levels:

Of the data so far recorded the most fascinating results have come from IQ readings. IQ, on average, drops by 10 full points after a

118

three-hour cycle ride. Manifestations of this include the extra-ordinary high level of inane banter and unalloyed merriment at the end of races – and the fact that even captains of industry will wait, exhausted, in the blazing sun for two hours for the mandatory after-race lucky-draw which offers prizes that no-one, who can afford a state-of-the-art bicycle, could conceivably want or need. At one recent event prizes included a set of jumper leads, a slide-rule, dinner with a DJ and a night for one in a Boksburg hotel.

A longer-term ambition of Chronosplit is to increase the diagnostic potential of the system's mats so that, from physiological data available from the start-mat, race winners could be determined before the race – as well as the winners of the lucky draw.

I realise one can't always believe what one reads in the pharmaceutical press but this does suggest an interesting trend.

The chicken hearts

A few years ago the Irish Tourist Board in Dublin (Bord Failte) and the Northern Ireland Tourist Board in Belfast decided to join forces and bring Ireland under one umbrella. There are now three bodies. But it makes sense because the third one – Tourism Ireland – is the overseas marketing arm of the two existing boards. It was Roger Cresswell and Helen Fraser – South African representatives of Tourism Ireland – who put the idea of cycling in Ireland into my head. We of the *Tour de Farce* had discussed it often for I had been greatly impressed by the tranquillity of Ireland, especially around its lakes and waterways, but we had been put off by the narrowness of the roads and the weather. The roads in fact proved perfect. The weather? We were about to see.

Tour de Farce IV was to begin on the coast of Northern Ireland 40km east of Belfast. We were to head north and, keeping roughly to the arc of the ragged northern coastline, and end 700-800km away at Westport near where the sun goes down on Galway Bay. Once more we had decided on the month of May for we all agreed May was the liveliest of months in Europe, being high spring and off-season, which meant fewer tourists and lower tariffs. One or two of my companions were worried about rain. I told them I had been to Ireland several times and experienced very few rainy days. 'Anyway, what's a little rain?' I said. 'Have we not cycled through sleet and snow and howling winds?'

'No,' they said.

Somebody added, 'It could rain for days on end. And mountain bikes don't have mudguards.'

'We will be using trek bikes – with mudguards,' I assured my chicken-hearted friend. 'In Ireland even old ladies without bikes have mudguards. But look here, are we sissies who are afraid of getting wet – or are we MEN?'

'Sissies,' they said.

'It's not just rain,' said Alan. 'I read that there are 360 golf courses in the Republic of Ireland and another 120 in Northern Ireland. If it isn't raining rain it's raining golf balls as big as our hailstones.'

'And how about the wind?' somebody asked. He added gloomily, 'We'll be cycling across the top of Ireland. Imagine a 50km/h headwind. Even if we pedal at 50km/h we'll be pedalling on the same spot all day.'

'But look on the bright side,' I said. 'It might be a 50km/h EASTERLY! Then we'd be able to do 50km in one hour without pedalling at all and have our noses deep into the Guinness by mid-morning.'

'Unless,' Alan said, 'we happen to be cycling down the west coast along the tops of those 300m-high cliffs with rocks at the bottom.'

'In which case we'll be reduced to high-protein puffin muffins,' said Rex.

Harvey, who'd been looking at maps, was worried about distances. He e-mailed to say, 'You tell us the first day will be a mere 40km from Ballygally to Ballycastle going via Ballyboy. It's more like bally 70km [*I was absolutely right! – Ed*] and to get there we have to cross a canyon on a rope bridge near Sheep's Island. That is according to my map – though I confess it's an Irish map.'

I was able to reassure him that last time I was there the road was perfectly smooth all the way and I certainly couldn't remember crossing a rope bridge. Roger Cresswell, who has cycled not only in Ireland but from India all the way to China, assured me that late May was a beautiful time to cycle through the Emerald Isle. The fields, he said, will sparkle with buttercups and daises, everything will be blossoming, 'and if you experience a spring shower just pop into a pub until it stops'.

Friendly pubs are part of the magic of Ireland. Jim Paul, head of Tourism Ireland, told me that he once spotted a notice outside a Northern Ireland pub: 'Come inside for a pint, a pie and a friendly word.' Jim went in and ordered a pint and a pie. The barman slid them across the counter and said that that would be five pounds. Jim said, 'What about the friendly word?' The barman leaned across the counter and whispered, 'Don't eat the pie.'

An added attraction to cycling round Ireland is that everybody speaks English so at least we wouldn't have to shout to make people understand as we had to in France and Italy and especially in Hungary where everybody has to shout to be understood. [*All the same some of us had difficulties. I recall the following conversation between our Leader and a local: 'Are you speaking Gaelic?'*

'No-noo, 'tis the Oirish we speak.'

'It sounds like Gaelic.'

''Tis you who calls it Gaelic, but in English we call it Irish.'

'Ah.'

– Ed]

My major problem remained the question of morale...

Rex in Hermanus, having seen the itinerary for the first time, e-mailed to say, 'I depart this evening partly to play golf in a distant town but mostly to recover from the shock of finding that I am committed to riding 60km a day around Ireland's rain-lashed hills. If that's light recreation, I'm an Irishman'.

It became incumbent upon me, as Leader, to stamp out this sort of morale-sapping nonsense. Where will we be if the team is going to fret about hills when those hills are still 10 000km away? How can they worry about rain before it even begins to lash at them, horizontally, blinding them and, day after day, soaking them through to their skins which will be puckered like raw tripe and with no chance of dry clothes until they get back to South Africa?

Daily the BBC weather reports for Ireland were more worrying. At this time of year nature usually waters Ireland daily but in short springtime showers followed by rainbows, bright sunshine, swallows sailing in a sunny sky and all that kind of stuff. Harvey didn't see it this way. With much figurative finger wagging he again warned via e-mail of rain and wind and the dreaded 'rope bridge across a canyon'. His alarmist stories – e-mailed to the entire team – were insensitive in view of the fact that the three younger members of the team were already grizzling and hand wringing. One of them, after all, was only 56 and hugely impressionable, and two others were barely into their sixties.

I discovered there is indeed a rope bridge but it was for pedestrians only – the Carrick-a-Rede Rope Bridge 30m above the sea near the Giant's Causeway. I told Harvey. But, ever alarmist, he changed tack and asked if we recalled the film *Ryan's Daughter* and the bleak coastal scenes of shrapnel-like rain and howling winds. Our cycle-hire man in Ireland, John Ahern, reassured us. He said those scenes were in fact shot in South Africa not far from where Harvey now lived. Nevertheless, the fear of rain continued to feature almost daily in e-mails and Harvey, who, by then, was already in Europe, cruising down the Danube on a conscience-appeasing holiday with Arlene, sent a last warning e-mail: 'My memory tells me that I issued a similar caution about rain before we set off down the Danube in May 2002. If conditions had been as I predicted – I would have been RIGHT! So be warned!'

In truth, I too was by now a little worried. I was alone in not worrying about rain but the other five, being native South Africans, were not used to getting wet and remaining wet, perhaps, all day. I e-mailed John Ahern in County Clare who was organising the details of our two weeks in Ireland and told him how the satellite view of Europe on Sky News weather reports had lately shown no sign of Ireland – just one great puddle as if a tsunami had swept clean across the island from the Atlantic. Should we postpone our tour for a month? John said, 'Do you really take weather forecasts seriously? Are you one of those people who believes what you read in the newspapers?'

The proof would be in the pudding.

The pudding

They say Belfast, capital of Northern Ireland, is in Ireland but not of it. I suppose one can say the same of many of the world's major cities – Johannesburg bears no resemblance at all to the rest of South

Africa, New York is quite different from the rest of the United States and London bears no resemblance to England. Architecturally Belfast is like Glasgow and they both look like Birmingham. A number of commentators have tried to define Belfast. It has a notorious past as a city torn apart ostensibly by religion although religion merely supplied the symbols. It is today an exciting place, a reborn city filled with optimism and activity and new attractions. It was in Belfast that the *Tour de Farce IV* mustered in May 2005. Harvey had flown in via Amsterdam and Rex had come in from Cape Town on a separate British Airways flight from those of us who had embarked in Johannesburg.

Travel writers sometimes travel – courtesy of the airline – business class or better. When travelling economy class they live in hope of an upgrade though they rarely get one these days. I normally feel a little guilty travelling business class or first class. I think it's the curtain that does it. The curtain in an airliner is the world's most unsubtle class barrier. At take-off the curtain between, say, business class and economy is left open. This is so that if the take-off is not to everybody's satisfaction – let's say the plane lands up in a cabbage field – the poor in economy can use the business class exit which I think is really jolly sporting of the people up front. One always knows when the crew is happy with the take-off because a stewardess immediately snaps the curtain closed, thus separating the hoi polloi from the upper crust. The curtain also, no doubt, avoids unseemly clashes between the haves and the have-nots by preventing a deep sense of deprivation building up in economy class as they see passengers up front relaxing in enormous recliners, being spoiled rotten by air hostesses popping grapes into their mouths.

All the same I must admit to a definite feeling of superiority when elevated to the superior front section which might even begin in the terminal itself as I crash my trolley through the economy class queues up to the red-carpeted, less pressured business and first class check-in desk. Here they place bright red PRIORITY labels on my bags and with deep respect direct me to the business lounge. There are armchairs in the business lounge and one gets free snacks and drinks and I sometimes have to be restrained. This agreeable feeling wells up again when I am ushered into the front section of the aircraft where they have reclining seats and offer French champagne and a hot towel before take-off. Sometimes I wonder how I'll ever be able to descend again to the level of my family and friends.

One shouldn't feel guilty of course. After all it's not just you who is getting a free ride. Nobody in business class or first class is paying. Businessmen charge the fare to the company and politicians and officials have their fares paid by the taxpayers sitting at the back. But sometimes, when in business class, I am overcome with compassion and a strong desire to scatter my superior business class cashew nuts among the peanut-eaters in economy class but I suppose this would simply cause an unseemly scramble – possibly even a mid-air riot. BA sensitively calls economy class 'tourist class'. Virgin Atlantic, waggling two fingers at the poor, calls its luxury section 'Upper Class' which infers that those on the wrong side of the curtain are lower class. I travelled Upper Class on Virgin once but all the time I knew, in my heart of hearts, that although those in the lower class looked inferior, some could quite possibly have been my equal, or nearly so.

We had flown on BA's intermediate class which mercifully gives extra leg room and Peter, in name-dropping mode, told us of a luxurious flight when he flew with Pérez de Cuéllar, the former UN chief, to Angola in the secretary-general's private 707 attended by a bevy of Iberian Airlines air hostesses – '10 females to each male passenger'.

Anyway, here we were again – not quite the full set of six. Alan, because of illness, had had to drop out on the day of our departure. We were gathered in Belfast's Wellington Park Hotel. I had asked the Northern Ireland tourist authority if they could get Ken McElroy as our guide for the afternoon. Ken is a historian and a very successful playwright on both sides of the Atlantic and I'd met him on a previous visit and had been impressed by his knowledge and objectivity in a city where objectivity in Northern Ireland was then as rare as warthogs. I was delighted when he pitched up at our hotel.

As we passed the city hall Ken told us a story that epitomises what is happening in Belfast. The story concerned Jimmy Magennis, VC. Magennis was a broth of a lad from Belfast who, during World War II, joined the Royal Navy and volunteered for a particularly dangerous night mission against the Japanese in Singapore harbour. He was made aware that capture meant death. He sat astride a miniature submarine, slid under the defences and placed limpet mines on the hulls of two ships. They failed to go off. So he went in a second time – and succeeded. He won the Victoria Cross for that, but back home he was met with tight-mouthed silence by the ruling Protestants because he was Catholic. Neither did the Catholics hail him for he had fought for the Protestant British. He died a disillusioned drunkard having sold his VC. Later an anonymous person bought the medal at an auction and returned it to his family. The city has since erected a monument in his honour outside the City Hall.

'The Troubles' are over – at least in their violent form – but the recent past is part of the fascination of visiting Northern Ireland. Belfast is a very English-looking city and an abiding memory is of huge murals and billboards depicting through Catholic and Protestant eyes the history of Ireland right up to the present. A few are provocative and all are aggrieved but mostly they call for an understanding and for tolerance and peace. The huge mural depicting the ten men, led by Bobby Sands, who starved themselves to death in the name of a united Ireland, is particularly poignant and there are beautifully inscribed verses and quotations – one quoting Sands: 'All things must come to pass. So hope will never die.' Many of the murals or billboards are massive – three storeys high – and the whole represents an historical milestone in art. Here are two bitterly opposed sides talking, at last, to each other in pictures, their swords transformed into paintbrushes. Rex described it as 'painting over deep-seated animosities'. The 'art war' has become a major tourist attraction, providing quite lucrative jobs for former fighters. Now that both sides have eschewed violence, tourism is breaking out all over Northern Ireland. Even the old docks are tourist sites. We visited the dry dock where the Titanic was built. The blocks upon which it stood on the slipway before being launched into history are still there. So is the captain's dinner table – it missed the boat. The locals, a little miffed that the world sees them as the makers of a ship that was so catastrophically flawed, try to assure visitors, 'It was fine when it left here!' But it wasn't of course.

Giants and giraffes

Next day dawned dull. It drizzled, spat and sometimes poured. We were picked up at the hotel by John Ahern who drove us to the coast in a minibus. John is the archetypal Irishman – bulky, red faced and prematurely grey – and full of amusing blarney. He arrived late in the morning which worried us because we had about 70km to cycle to our first night's stop, Ballycastle, and still had to get to the starting point, Ballygally. It was quite a drive and there was nothing much there except a quaint hotel, lots of gannets, black-headed gulls, oyster-catchers and John's service van standing in a puddle in the car park – and six not terribly new bicycles. There was a lot of fiddling: bikes to be tested, saddles needing adjusting, handlebars tightening; somebody had lost his gloves. But we then peeled off our tracksuits, put on our crash helmets and stood there shivering in the wind and intermittent light rain while even more adjustments were made.

Despite it all, once we were off – it was already noon – we made good time along the winding and attractive coastal road. The wind was behind us and the sun occasionally broke through and we all felt in fine fettle and in buoyant mood. I decided against wearing rain gear because cycling shirts dry out as quickly as one's skin and I knew that our exertions, mild as they were on this mostly flat road, would soon make us warm. After an hour or so and having climbed one of the few long hills – this one led out of Cushendall – we noticed two of our team were missing. From the hilltop through binoculars I spotted Peter and Rex three kilometres back mending a flat tyre. It was taking so long we decided to go back and help. That was when we discovered Peter's wheel was badly buckled. And we'd all forgotten over the years how to take a back wheel off without dismantling the gears. In any event the bikes of our childhood, if they had any gears at all, had three-phase gears which were unsophisticated. We noticed that Harvey's wheel was also buckled. We called John's back-up man on the cell phone but continued to ride slowly for another 20km where the service van met us and changed the two bikes.

We cycled on to Cushendun where we abandoned the coast and headed inland straight towards our first night's stop even though it meant an 8km zig-zagging climb. I was delighted to find I could climb it without dismounting though I remained way behind the rest. As we climbed higher the varied coastal vegetation gave way to treeless tussock country and the elevation added to the cold but it was worth the climb for we had dramatic views down to the sea. By now it was raining but we were now able to freewheel for at least five or six kilometres even though frozen to the marrow by the chill of a blustery wind. Perversely, this is what made it so enjoyable – arriving in Ballycastle at the warm and welcoming Marine Hotel whose staff had reserved separate rooms for us so that nobody had to wait a moment longer than necessary for a hot bath. Under such circumstances to have hot bath and change into dry warm clothes and then sit down to a robust Irish meal is one of life's most satisfying pleasures.

Rex in an article in Carol Lazar's *Travel* section of the *Saturday Star* put the pleasures of such cycling more plainly: 'It's so nice when you stop.'

We were up at dawn and were greeted by bright sunshine and a bitterly cold wind. I left before the others because there was a long steep hill out of town and I didn't want anybody to wait for me at the top in the polar wind. Once at the top I leaned against a stone wall watching a flock of fat sheep and the blue sea beyond. Ireland is good for the eyes. I then noticed Rex and Harvey were also walking up. Despite the threat of rain and the cold I again decided not to wear a rain cape reasoning that I would get just as wet from sweat as from the rain.

We arrived at Harvey's dreaded Carrick-a-Rede Rope Bridge. It was well off the road and was reached by a long, steep descent on foot. We were richly rewarded. The swaying bridge links the mainland to an island with high cliffs all around. Wherever one looks the coastal scenery is dramatic but what was unforgettable was seeing, 30m below, razorbills flying their peculiar fluttering flight just above the waves and then diving into the sea to resume flying beneath the surface. They look like miniature flying penguins which in many ways they are. Colourful vetches – legumes that make good fodder – shone in the sunshine along the footpath.

I had now given up trying to appear rugged and gratefully accepted Richard's offer of a rain cape (he was wearing a windcheater). The cape had a monk-like hood and upon this I sat my helmet – a sight that, I noticed, badly frightened children. We visited the nearby Giants Causeway which Richard, with his gammy knee, refused to clamber over and so he never witnessed to the full

127

this astonishing piece of coastal geomorphology seemingly constructed out of 38 000 interlocked hexagonal basalt columns, some 12m tall. Against the mainland there is a 6km arc of towering 'fluted' cliffs reminiscent of a giant cathedral organ. Geologists say the causeway was caused 60 million years ago by cooling lava but the locals' version sounds more plausible – a giant, Finn MacCool, built it so he could walk to Scotland and give supergiant, Benandonner, a fright. Samuel Johnson said the causeway was 'worth seeing but not worth going to see'. (Johnson can often be wrong of course – his 1755 *Dictionary* states that female elephants make love lying on their backs. He was right though about giraffes: 'The giraffe is taller than the elephant but not so thick.')

We arrived at the ancient Bushmills Inn, cosy, creaky and rustic and there we bought a bottle of Bushmills whiskey between us and sat in front of the hearth to savour it. We were amazed at how quickly it went. Rex said it was due to evaporation caused by the inn's peat-burning hearth.

Next day the rain came down in curtains and John Ahern, realising he had underestimated the distance we were to cycle that day (our 11-day route was, after all, experimental) sent a coach to take us as far as Limavady from where we were to cycle south, deep inland, through the Sperrin Mountains on a circuitous 100km route to Londonderry. But the weather was so bad that after three hours' cycling, and realising the mountains would be hidden anyway, we gave up the scenic route and took the busy main road directly to Londonderry. Cold and wet, we reached the river Foyle around 6 pm. Sixty years ago the entire German U-boat fleet sailed down this river to surrender to the British at Londonderry's naval base at the end of World War II.

Our instruction said we should cross the Foyle Bridge using the lower section but, having battled up a long ramp through bumper-to-bumper traffic, we found the bridge, under repair, had no lower section and in any event cyclists were barred. We were told to cross a bridge many kilometres lower down – a double-decker bridge. The rain now fell steadily and it was getting dark when we finally crossed the bridge and spotted the welcoming sight of Londonderry's big, warmly lit City Hotel where the manager, Colin Ahern (son of John) greeted us as only the Irish can and invited us to dinner.

128

All night the wind lashed the city and the rain drummed against my window. It was no better in the morning. All the same, as the hotel was next to the city wall I put on a rain cape and walked clean around Derry – which is built on a hill – along the top of the wall. It's less than two kilometres and is well worth the effort for, among other things, one has an interesting view of the inner city and of what lies outside. At one point one looks down into 'Catholic Bogside' with its row houses and skillfully done murals on the sides of some homes depicting tragic moments in Bogside's recent past. There's the Penny Cathedral – 'built with the pennies of the poor' – which contrasts with the Protestant cathedral inside the wall built by funds from across the Irish Sea. The one is full every Sunday, the other quiet.

Blood, sweat and beers

John phoned during breakfast. It would be madness, he said, to cycle in the gale and the rain that was sweeping across the top of Ireland and he sent a coach to take us to our next stop – Rathmullen on Lough Swilly. We welcomed this but it was a great shame because the coastline is dramatic and there would have been so much to see of historical interest. Two hours later the coach turned through the gates of a magnificent Georgian mansion – Rathmullen House, our B&B. The sun suddenly beamed down and we celebrated its appearance with a memorable lunch and what the English would call a bracing walk along the gale-lashed lough. The next day dawned bright and clear, though still bitterly cold. I walked through the gardens disturbing the rabbits which were out in force with their young. Down at the quayside I met a local woman walking her dog who told me this was the wettest May she could remember in the 40 years she had lived in Northern Ireland.

There is that charming Irish blessing: 'May the road rise up to meet you, and the wind be always on your back.' Five kilometres south of Rathmullen, with the wind on our backs and the sun shining warmly, the road did its duty and rose up to meet me. The tool bag fell off my handlebars in front of my wheel and all 95kg of me rocketed forward and I came down on my left knee onto the newly tarred road. My knee was a nasty mess, a marble-sized stone briefly embedded beneath the kneecap. Peter later described to me in Technicolor and Stereophonic Sound how I had rolled over and how the back of my head hit the tarmac. Miraculously, I never felt a thing and because of my Bell helmet (rush out and buy one) I didn't even have to comb my hair afterwards. I had the bottle of eau de Cologne I had been carrying since the Danube and poured it into the gaping hole. Recalling Harvey's stoicism when he came a cropper in Italy I bound my knee with a handkerchief and, having reassured my steed, I remounted. An hour or so later we found a pharmacist in Rathmelton – Tom Murray – who was just about to go out with his family for it was Sunday. But he cheerfully opened his pharmacy, poured iodine into the wound and bound it more impressively. He said there was nothing that could be stitched for a piece of flesh was missing.

Later that morning, once more in intermittent rain, we ran up against the mother of all hills leading up to the village of Churchill, a settlement that was little more than a name on a map but it had a marvellous old pub at the summit where we had lunch. At one point I had to go outside to retrieve something from my pannier bag and was amazed to feel the heat of the sun. And there it was high in the sky doing what it was paid to do – shining. I was surprised the locals hadn't come rushing in to tell us.

The afternoon was spent in warm sunshine climbing forever upwards through the grassy Glendowan Mountains. It was worth the climb for the mountains, totally treeless, were spectacular and the sun spotlighted their wet, glistening, granite peaks. Around every corner we expected the road to summit only to be confronted by yet another long climb. Eventually we went over the top and had a breathtaking view down into a far lake-filled valley stage-lit by sunbeams. The sun shone warmly as we coasted for a considerable time before reaching the tree line and the odd farmhouse.

Once in the valley the road became a roller coaster and on one of the inclines we overtook, with some difficulty, a pair of tough old Dutch hikers who were walking at quite a pace. A few minutes later my handlebars suddenly became loose and the front wheel no longer responded to my steering. It would have been a tricky situation had we been going downhill. While we were repairing the bike the hikers overtook us. Later we overtook them – again on an incline. Then we had to stop again for adjustments. The hikers overtook us but out of politeness pretended they hadn't seen us. It is embarrassing being overtaken by hikers when you are mounted on a bicycle. We later overtook them and after that we didn't dare stop until we reached our night's stop at the Highland Inn in Glenties.

At the Highland Inn the manager, on seeing my gory leg, summoned on her own initiative a nursing sister named Carol who expertly cleaned and dressed my knee. Carol told me she worked at a nearby psychiatric hospital – 'I'm just round the bend,' she said explaining she was more used to dealing with people's heads than anything lower down. I told her how fortuitous it was because I was seriously worried about my companions' heads. She said she had spotted a couple of my companions in the foyer and there was very little she could do for people once they had reached the stage they appeared to have reached. When I asked how much I owed she laughed and said, 'For what?'

It was a pleasant hotel, no frills, but Richard found a plaque on his door saying that Meryl Streep had slept there. Maybe it now reads Meryl Streep and Richard Steyn slept here. That evening we had the definitive seafood chowder for which the Highland Inn was justifiably famous.

Next day we cycled no more than 35km to Donegal and had difficulty finding our B&B – a house in the suburbs. Peter, being a broth of a boy, sought out the prettiest girl he could find and asked directions.

'Never heard of it,' said she. 'Do you know its whereabouts?'

'It's in Ireland,' growled Rex who had been listening.

'Then you're in the right place!' said she gaily, and waved goodbye.

I recalled Jim Paul telling me about somebody asking an Irishman the quickest way to Tipperary. The man said, 'Would yer be travellin' by car or by foot?'

'Car.'

'Aye – that's the quickest way.'

I had the feeling my companions had taken the shortest route for my sake although they denied it. That evening we cycled back into town for dinner and while I felt little discomfort while pedalling I found it painful getting on and off the bike. Next day I felt it would be foolish to cycle and so took a country bus to our next stop, Sligo.

The distances John Ahern had guessed were what one would call very rough. A 60km ride would turn out to be 100 or more. The Irish are still in that confused state that inevitably follows after a country changes from miles to kilometres. They are also not hot on time. A 'ten-minute walk' can well be a half-hour slog. As Rex later wrote, 'The true charm of the Irish is that they have risen above the tyranny of time and space; perhaps even above mundane reality too. In the midst of modernity and prosperity they have, Hobbit-like, managed to preserve the quaintness of their own Middle Earth.'

Cycling by bus

Leadership is difficult at the best of times, especially when sitting in a rural bus. It says a lot for my companions that from that point on they never got themselves lost. I was filled with admiration that they could achieve this without my leadership and when, one evening, I expressed the thought that I might try to cycle with them they were shocked that I should take such a risk, warning me that I could wreck my knee for life and would spend my dotage persistently falling over. They fought with each other to pay my bus fare. I told them their generosity warmed my heart and said how proud I was of them now that they had the confidence to carry on without me. My little speech was enthusiastically received.

Harvey, who had arrived in Ireland with a dose of 'flu, took a turn for the worse and was also prevailed upon not to cycle that day. He joined me on the bus, our cycles stowed in the hold. On arrival in Sligo Harvey discovered he'd lost his rain jacket. Hurrying to replace it, we entered old-fashioned drapers, Mullany's Drapery Emporium. Harvey told the salesman that he did not want an expensive replacement, for he'd probably lose it again. The salesman produced one 'at half the price', and read aloud its label: 'Guaranteed water-proof. All materials guaranteed.' The salesman's eyes widened. 'You're not going to believe this,' he exclaimed. 'It says here "Guaranteed un-lose-able!"'

'I believe you,' said Harvey.

'Congratulations. You're the only man in Ireland who will,' he beamed. Harvey shared the news of this unbelievably valuable guarantee with the manager who was standing at the door in his smart, pinstriped suit and carefully shot cuffs and his response came in a twinkle: 'Ah, but our experience is that in 104 percent of these cases, it is not the jacket that is lost, but its owner.'

The quick and the sick

What with Alan having to cancel the tour because of illness, then me having had to retire hurt, and now Harvey incapacitated, the peloton was down to three. They made a sad sight from the bus. As we passed them pedalling in the rain we signalled encouragement from the bus window. Rex made a sign.

We were now in the Republic of Ireland – not that there are any borders. Ireland is Ireland these days. You know you're in the Republic only when the currency changes.

Two days later, having given up any thought of resuming cycling, I left my bike to be picked up by the back-up van and caught the luggage taxi to the Belmullet peninsula on Ireland's dramatic far west coast. The peninsula was a more or less treeless, windswept spit of land buffeted on one side by the North Atlantic and on the other by the choppy Black Sod Bay. The taxi driver pulled up at a shed next to the beach and to my amazement, as if on cue, a young woman in scuba kit stepped out of the sea and walked towards us. The driver asked if she knew Josephine Geraghty, the owner of the B&B where we were to spend the night. The diver said she had just arrived from England and knew nobody in the area. I wanted to ask her whether she'd swum around the north or around the south of Ireland on her way from England. It turned out there was a diving school on Black Sod Bay. We were by now halfway down the peninsula which is mainly marshland and learned there were three Josephine Geraghtys in this sparsely populated area – three unrelated Josephines had, many years ago, each married one of the Geraghty boys.

Josephine's B&B turned out to be a big, warm, modern and comfortable house set back from a small village and from my upstairs room I had a panoramic view of the bleak peninsula and the wide bay which was in a bad mood with scudding clouds and white horses. Far across the bay to the south I could just make out the misty grey bulk of Achill Island whose hills rise to almost 700m. The island was next day's destination and it was a good 100km by road.

133

My companions meanwhile were pedalling through rain across quite desolate landscapes. I was sorry I was missing out for I (seriously) enjoy wide-open spaces – even if they are bleak – and enjoy the taste of rain. Harvey, who was now back with them, described seeing, 'rising above the mist, great windmills, too tall even for a Don Quixote to tackle'. They were providing the clean electric energy that used to be produced by the world's only peat-fired power station, now standing derelict.

Harvey later wrote, 'Not a soul was to be seen on any of the mystic horizons stretching in all directions. On our left was a sign reading: 'To Black Sod', and that was the route we chose. Suddenly we came upon a strange bridge – the Musical Bridge whose story is a three-beer story – and just beyond it we tumbled out of the pelting rain into a warm pub, so welcome it even offered indoor shelter to our bikes. The unfinished musical bridge earned its name from the fact that its stones emit ringing tones when struck. It is unfinished because the local man who was paid to build it absconded with the money before it was complete. There is a curse involved somewhere in the story but Harvey had forgotten the details except that it is said to be the reason why three men who were called in to complete the job died one by one. An inspector who was sent to investigate the matter also died suddenly. After that nobody was keen on finishing the bridge.

By all accounts my companions had a tough ride well in excess of 100km and would have to retrace at least a quarter of the route next morning in order to clear the neck of the peninsula and then they'd have to cycle for some hours through featureless bogland.

While waiting for them to arrive I decided it would be sensible to take my knee for a walk. It had developed the habit of suddenly giving way. I had a long walk and, even though the weather was not terribly pleasant, I enjoyed every minute. Black Sod Bay, despite its name, is attractive and certainly exhilarating. I watched seagulls being thrown about the sky.

That evening we had the choice of cycling 13km in the rain to Belmullet village for dinner or paying the incredible sum of 40 Euros to go by taxi. We did the incredible.

To save the cyclists backtracking next day in the rain and wind Josephine arranged for her fishing boat to ferry us and our bikes to the island. It was, to say the least, a hair-raising crossing. The small boat punched its way through heavy swells and many a green sea crashed over our bows. There was a small bus waiting to take me to the hotel. Rex decided to join me. The others braved the head-on wind and cycled the 12km through what turned out to be beautiful, almost tropical, scenery to the Ostan Oilean Acla, a cosy quayside hotel. Ostan Oilean Acla is Gaelic, I think, for 'Come in but close that bloody door!' Because the bus, owned by two pensioners also served as the island's ambulance, school bus and shoppers' shuttle, the driver took a circuitous route, picking up and dropping people, so that we arrived at the hotel only a few minutes before our three colleagues. They entered, boasting loudly of their heroism. We celebrated another rugged day over a pint of Guinness and hot, golden chips.

A waitress told us that she had heard on TV that the next day would be sunny and would reach 19 degrees.

'Nineteen degrees!'

'Yes,' she said, 'people will be dropping like flies'.

We left the island next day before people began dropping and the sun, as advertised on TV, did indeed appear.

Our 11-day cycle ride ended in a beautiful little town, Westport, where we stayed in a charming 18th century hotel, the Olde Railway Hotel whose lounge was reminiscent of a traditional London club. So in fact was my Victorian bedroom.

From that day on the sun shone daily across Ireland with, no doubt, people dropping everywhere.

In retrospect we should have spent half the time in Northern Ireland and then got on a train and started the second half from around Galway Bay cycling south where the weather is much kinder – which is more or less what Tourism Ireland suggested to us in the first place.

But, as I said earlier, perversely the rain made our trip. Maybe it was because we are Highvelders who don't see a lot of rain but I think it was more because there's a great deal of pleasure in cycling slowly in soft rain – and it was mainly soft – and arriving at a warm village pub knowing that you have unquestionably earned the Guinness that the barman is slowly building for you. They don't just *pour* Guinness in Ireland; they build it up layer by layer with a reverence you don't come across apart from in factories where they bottle nitroglycerine.

On some days we barely stopped except for a pint of Guinness here and a pint of Guinness there and a thick Irish sandwich or two and the occasional spirited debate (over another Guinness) about the choice of routes. This was 'coarse cycling' at its best – the leisurely art of cycling along country roads – talking, shouting, pointing out to each other interesting or beautiful features. And each evening, after a hot bath and donning warm clothes, glowing with self-righteousness, we'd talk. One evening I mentioned how when I had last arrived in Dublin there was a red carpet at my feet leading all the way into the terminal. I was amazed at this reception because although I knew the Irish were very welcoming it was, after all, only my fourth visit. Bill Clinton had landed just before me so I suppose he, lucky fellow, was also able to walk on the red carpet. Peter mentioned he had met Clinton four times – once with his senatorial wife Hillary. He thought Bill, Nelson Mandela and Tony O'Reilly were the most charming of all the people he has met.

One morning, halfway through the trip, wet but cheerful and enjoying a well-earned rest in an ancient flagstoned inn, Richard said, 'I think we have come of age as cyclists.' We raised our glasses to that and to many other profound thoughts that I should have written down.

Chapter Nine

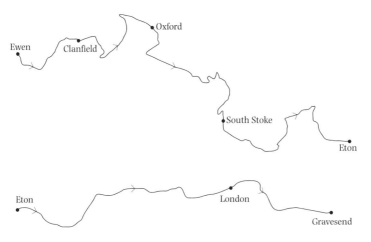

All tourists are essentially explorers otherwise they'd stay at home straightening pictures on the wall and letting the cat in and out. It was certainly with exploration in mind that, in planning *Tour de Farce V,* I approached the offices of VisitBritain (formerly the British Tourist Authority) in Hyde Park, Johannesburg. I reminded them that the year 2006 marked the 150th anniversary of the Burton-Speke Nile expedition which departed from Britain to find the source of Africa's most important river. It seemed appropriate, I said, that we from Africa embark on a cycle-mounted expedition to explore Britain's most important river – the Thames. There is, believe it or not, still some controversy over its source. Even Jerome K Jerome's famous Thames expedition, recounted in *Three Men in a Boat* in 1889, didn't venture very far into the mysterious interior of the West Country where the river's source is said to be.

Just as the Royal Geographic Society in Victorian times fell in with proposals by Burton, Speke, Stanley and others to explore Africa, so VisitBritain threw all their expertise into helping us work on a plan to explore the Thames and open up for the public the wonders of the Valley from its source to the North Sea. They suggested we make our base camp the 500-year-old Wild Duck Inn in the village of Ewen near Cirencester. This, my colleagues agreed, sounded an excellent idea. Edwin Swan and Elmarie Hall who head VisitBritain in Johannesburg, said one of the supposed sources of the Thames was only 6km from there.

Once again there was the advantage that the people of the Thames Valley are known to speak a form of English. Admittedly their pronunciation can sometimes puzzle. If, for instance, you ask a West Country man, 'Kind sir, is this the way to Bicester?' (they pronounce it 'bister' just as they pronounce Gloucester, 'Gloster' and Worcester 'Wooster') he will say, 'Eee-arrr' which, in West Country patois means, 'Yes'.

Another attraction is that the valley is not only beautiful but, as somebody long ago said, 'Every drop is liquid 'istory.' Its colourful story involves kings and queens, knaves, battles, Romans, Saxons, Druids, stormy royal love affairs, West Ham United and many bizarre customs. There's even *pre*'istory in that there are intriguing clues to life in the valley going back to the time when the Thames was still a tributary of the Rhine. It stopped being a tributary when the Ice Age melted and the English Channel formed 10 056 years ago. (I know the precise date because when I was at school we were told Britain became separated from the Continent when the Ice Age melted 10 000 years ago.) And there are signs of Romans everywhere. That goes for the whole of England of course but particularly the Thames. People are constantly coming across Roman coins (why were the Romans so careless with their money?) and archaeologists are excavating Roman sites by the score. Cirencester – called Corinium in Roman times when it was Britain's second-largest city after London – is built upon Roman ruins. A few years ago, archaeologists excavated an enormous Roman fort called Vindolanda which, although not in the Thames Valley, gave a fascinating insight into how the Romans felt about being in Britain. Scores of letters and notes were unearthed written in ink on wafer-thin pieces of wood the size of postcards. The messages indicated that Roman soldiers were, according to scholars, 'preoccupied with socialising and writing letters home begging their parents to send luxuries'. One letter challenged the image that Romans were master road-builders. It was signed by a Roman named Octavius and inferred that the Romans hated the English weather and, surprisingly, that because of the climate the Roman-built roads weren't fit for wheeled traffic. I am not in the habit of reading other people's mail but I can guess what it said ...

Vindolanda Mars XV

Dearest Mama,

It has not stopped raining since Septem and my skin is all white and crinkly. My helmet has half-a-XII rust spots and my leather skirt is green with mildew. I beseech you, Mama, please send me some olive oil, a new toga, some vino and some money.

Our civil engineers are having a bad time building roads. Because of the weather the roads quickly become quagmires and the local savages have taken to them like ducks to water – they trundle up and down with their infernal herds and their crude ox-sleds which cause massive congestion. Yesterday I was stuck in an hour-long chariot jam on the MV, the new route to Londinium. O Jupiter! All those horses and cattle and ox-carts, cattle pads and horse droppings! By the time traffic eased the malodorous pollution was axle deep and steaming like Vesuvius.

The placid Druids, who are quite creepy, say these gaseous odours will eventually change the climate causing Britain to become warmer and as dry as the Sahara. Flavius says the Druids are insanely optimistic.

The worst drivers are women although there are not many of them. Down in Londinium there is one, a warrior named Boadicea, who has it in for us. Instead of hubcaps on her chariot she has curved knives and races through our garrisons whipping off kneecaps – and worse with the shorter fellows.

She is typical of the locals – they resent all we do for them. They seem to forget that until we arrived they had no idea what a shovel was! The Picts are not bad though. Flavius says that with C Picts and C shovels he could construct IV kilometres of roads per diem.

139

I cannot wait to get home and am ever grateful that your wise counsel led me to invest all my dinars in that little townhouse in Pompeii. At least there is no air pollution there.

Hail Caesar and all that,
Octavius.

PS Don't forget the money. I really don't know where all my coins go.

Gentle cycling

Once again, wearing the mantle of Leader I had the onerous responsibility to lead my five faithful companions into the unknown and bring them safely back to their loved ones, if any. What was, in 2002, a once-off idea had now become, like the *Tour de France* itself, firmly established as an annual event. Why were we doing it? We were still uncertain. As Lance Armstrong said, 'It's not about the bike.' That much we knew. Alan thought it was more about the stomach.

The Thames is only 338km long. That's not far, I can hear you say. After all, the Eastern Cape has earthworms longer than that. I can only repeat that I do wish readers would refrain from interrupting. [*It must be very irritating. —Ed*] Yet to cycle from the Thames' source to its estuary was to take a week of steady pedalling and re-fuelling on low-octane English ale from which beverage we were, nevertheless, able to achieve 35km a litre.

Our route and stopovers were organised by a Buckinghamshire company, Capital Sports, whose motto was, 'Gentle Cycling'. The lads squirmed with embarrassment when I mentioned 'Gentle Cycling' for although our average age was by now 68 we were a rugged bunch who, even in the South African winter could sometimes be seen outside without jerseys.

There was even more shuffling of the feet when I broke the news that after the Thames we were going to cross to France for a week-long celebratory tour of the Lower Loire Valley – to celebrate the completion of our fifth expedition. This I had booked through a widely known UK group called 'Cycling for Softies' which specialises in cycling in France. Our old friend in Cape Town, Serena

THAMES VALLEY

TOP LEFT: Stone marking the supposed eye of the Thames. Rex said one can no longer believe everything that is cast in stone. BELOW LEFT: About to start the Thames expedition – a little later we found ourselves back at this spot. CENTRE: Colourful rape seed (canola) has transformed rural scenery across Britain and the Continent. INSET: Strategising at the Wild Duck Inn with Capital Sports' Wendy Carter the day before assaulting the Thames. BELOW: The Plough at Clanfield.

Tour de Farce V – Thames Valley

TOP & INSET: The Thames becomes navigable from Lechlade where these pictures were taken. The upper valley was once deep forest felled by the Romans when building London.
CENTRE & BELOW: The Thames Path often reverts to a narrow footpath.

Tour de Farce V – Thames Valley

TOP: The trout-filled upper Thames. CENTRE LEFT: Climbing out of a forest detour (even Richard Steyn had to walk) and negotiating one of the frequent stiles (to stop cattle straying). RIGHT: We thought Harvey was throwing up – his sunglasses had fallen in the river and he was hoping a fish would return them. BELOW: We were often directionally challenged especially when our Cycling Lab shirts blended with the rape fields.

Tour de Farce V – Thames Valley

The coach yard at the George Inn in Dorchester. CENTRE: The Oxford pub where many great authors met – locally known as the Bird & Baby. BELOW: Our last day on the Thames – with 75km ahead of us. It began grey and ended greyer as we approached the North Sea.

Tour de Farce V – Thames Valley

LOIRE VALLEY

TOP: Dragging our luggage from the station at Chinon to begin a week-long ride in the Loire Valley. MIDDLE: Astride our steeds ready to begin the second stage of Tour de Farce V. ABOVE: Joan of Arc in irritable mood. BELOW: Tackling a yard of ale. It was amazing how fast it went after four hours of cycling.

Tour de Farce V – Loire Valley

TOP: Part of the ancient hostelry of Le Vieux Chateau, where we stayed at Hommes, and its baronial dining room where Mme Hardy prepared a memorable dinner. CENTRE: The chateau at Villandry and, BELOW, its famous gardens where even cabbages grow where they are told.

Tour de Farce V – Loire Valley

TOP: It never ceased to amaze me how easy it was to get lost following a river. ABOVE: Even on a road with no junctions some of us were sometimes unsure which way to go. INSET: Harvey meets a Rolls Royce manufactured in the year he too was manufactured.

Tour de Farce V – Loire Valley

TOP: I can't recall how it was that we found ourselves in a wood. CENTRE: A chateau on the Indre River. INSET: A glimpse of what the smart cyclist was wearing in the Spring of 2006. BELOW: The Tour de Farce V team enjoys a farewell drink back at Chinon where we had begun.

Tour de Farce V – Loire Valley

Cartwright, who represents Cycling for Softies, had organised it. She said 'Softies' do everything for you except pedal. I had to remind her that we were not softies. She said she fully understood, but what did we expect Cycling for Softies to do – change its name to Cycling for Toughies?

There were the usual misgivings when we discussed the finer details of the Thames expedition. Only days before we were due to leave, Richard e-mailed to ask if I'd seen the current temperatures along the Thames Valley. They were as low as 1° C. Even our campaign-hardened photographer, Alan, was worried about his pixels freezing. I told them to pull themselves together. It will be the Merry Month of May, the height of springtime in England.

To save time we decided to fly the first 10 000km from Johannesburg, once again using a British Airways aeroplane. BA agreed to drop us off at London's Heathrow Airport which, they pointed out, is in the Thames Valley from where Capital Sports would bus us to Ewen where our bikes were tethered and the Thames eye was waiting to be discovered.

The hole in the ground

We found Cirencester a pleasant little city and we visited its ancient cathedral built centuries ago by the wool barons of the Cotswolds. The contrast between Britain's austere and poorly illuminated cathedral interiors and Europe's flamboyant basilicas with their hallelujah gilded statues and unrestrained baroque ornamentation is profound and says a lot about the differences between Continentals and the Brits though I am not sure what. Accompanied by Wendy Carter who had met us at Heathrow Airport and who is a guide with Capital Sports, and Mike Dunmore, an Oxford-based guide (he is also Capital Sport's Mr Fixit) we then drove a few kilometres from Cirencester to some undulating farmland near the village of Ewen, whose name means 'river source'. We stopped at an open farm gate from where we walked a kilometre or so over a knoll and down into a pretty glade with a copse whose floor was covered in bluebells. Here Wendy pointed out a shallow, bath-sized depression of exposed limestone. An adjacent slab of engraved Cotswold rock proclaimed that this was it – this was the source of the Thames – 'Thameshead'.

141

It was bone dry. We found it very hard to believe that this was the eye of Britain's most famous river. Rex said the world had come to a pretty pass when one could no longer believe what one read engraved in stone. We stared at the hole for as long as seemed appropriate before trudging back over the knoll.

There are people who say that the Thames' real source is a few kilometres north of Cirencester a little south of Cheltenham. This is where the River Churn rises. The Churn, at an elevation ever so slightly higher than the Thames, joins the Thames east of Cirencester and many people say the Thames should be renamed the Churn. Anyway the Thames is properly called the Isis all the way down river until it passes Oxford. In Oxford itself people hiss if you refer to the river as the Thames. It is always the Isis. We found this all very confusing and, as we'd forgotten to bring a tape measure to measure distances and as it was practically lunchtime, we unanimously agreed to repair to the Wild Duck Inn. As Rex said, 'It's all too much.' We hurried to the Wild Duck where, with Wendy and Mike, we dined in a cosy corner of the ancient tavern and discussed the week that lay ahead. My mind wandered off on its own, as it so often does, and I thought about earlier customers who had sat in this very corner of the tavern, centuries ago, debating even weightier matters – matters such as whether the earth was flat and whether you'd fall off the edge if you sailed too far out to sea and whether inserting tadpoles into the ear was a genuine cure for the Black Plague or whether it was just another apothecary's trick to sell tadpoles.

We ordered our first English pint of ale and solemnly raised our glasses to the *Tour de Farce* 2006.

The Wild West

On day one, as titular leader, it was my duty to head the pack as we left the front of the inn where we had dined so well and spent a comfortable night (me in a four-poster bed). I led the peloton smoothly into the first turn left as instructed by the guidebook and a few minutes later we found ourselves back outside the Wild Duck Inn, this time behind it. This triggered a number of comments, none of them particularly helpful. I realised that the instructions assumed we would have cycled off from *behind* the inn in which case the first left would have been the correct turn. Fortunately, once we were on the right road we managed to cycle a fair distance – at least two kilometres – before again becoming disoriented. We cycled back to the last turn only to discover we were right first time. So we retraced our tracks. But again it did not seem right so we again pedalled back. We got to know the farms along this stretch of road quite intimately and they got to know us.

In case the reader might think we were stupid or at least directionally challenged I should point out that we have little or no trouble at all when pedalling along straight roads. It's when a road forks or there's a T-junction that everybody starts arguing and then out come the maps and voices begin to rise. When three or four roads come together it is, as you can imagine, sheer hell. Richard, who can't even refold a map properly let alone bother to read one, will set his heart on a direction and might even pedal off, thus forcing the issue. Rex will growl dissent whichever route we choose. Harvey will tear his hair – mainly because he is the only one with any hair to speak of – and use words that I'm sure his wife never hears. Peter will shout orders like an *obergruppenführer*. Alan tends to stand back knowing that to add a fifth voice would be pointless. I sometimes join in – like a dog that is set off barking when it hears other dogs barking – and I shout things just for the fun of it. Thus we disturbed many a village that had otherwise been at peace since Saxon times.

Peter, who by now had reached the ripe old age of 57, would often clutch his head and reel about at all this doddering and again and again I needed to remind him that to remain one of us he had to learn to dodder down a great deal more. On the road he often raced up and down our strung-out column as if he were a cavalry outrider warning of an imminent Apache attack. Rex said we should pop Ritalin into his breakfast tea.

The upper Thames runs an intensely beautiful course, sometimes through tunnels of willows, sometimes surging through broad water meadows patrolled by swans the size of Volkswagens and flotillas of Canada geese. The grass verges along the country lanes were filled with wild flowers and from the roadside drainage ditches sprouted cowslips (marsh marigolds) like giant buttercups to which they are related. The sun beamed down on us.

We were in no hurry and spent a great deal of time leaning

over wooden bridges admiring Monet-like water lily scenes. At one bridge Harvey remained leaning over for some time and we had to go back for him. We thought he was throwing up for he was leaning right over. But no. He had been looking over the parapet when his posh wrap-around sunglasses fell from his head into deep water. He was gloomily staring at the spot where they had disappeared hoping that a trout might pop up with them. Somebody asked him, 'Did you make a wish?'

By midday we had lost three of our companions but Peter, Harvey and I pedalled on for some time doing a bit of birding in the wetlands. The water meadows gave way to open farmland and the Thames matured into a definable river that at last seemed to know where it was going. There had been nary a hill the entire day and we were cruising at 15km/h, taking lots of wrong turns, when we spotted an irresistible sign pointing off our route to the south. It read 'The Red Lion – first pub on the Thames'. We turned off in that wordless, synchronised way we had perfected and soon found ourselves in a quaint village, Castle Eaton, on the banks of the river. At the Red Lion we barely had time to dip our noses into a glass of ale when in walked our lost friends.

For three quarters of its length there is a path along the Thames, a path for cyclists as well as hikers and horse riders. Indeed it was once a towpath though now that the barge horses have gone it has become very narrow in parts – so narrow and so deeply recessed from constant use by hikers that both Rex and I were soon thrown from our mounts into the grass as our wheels became trapped as if in a tramline. This is why for the first couple of days we chose to cycle along the smooth country lanes, some bearing the sign, 'Quiet Road', which meant cars were not allowed to knock cyclists down, not that I recall seeing any cars.

There is a voluntary organisation in Britain known as Sustrans ('Sustainable Transport') dedicated to expanding a national cycle path network and marked by blue bicycle signs. So far it comprises 16 000km of traffic-free routes and designated 'quiet roads' and, through cities, 'traffic-calmed' roads. Every Englishman is within 3km of that network. Thanks to Sustrans' campaign and the co-operation of local authorities we were almost never in conflict with traffic. We were in conflict with cows and gates and stiles, yes, but never traffic – until we reached London, but even there drivers were very considerate.

We began spotting road signs to places with familiar names – Wantage, for instance, made famous by that saucy limerick:

There was a young lady of Wantage
Of whom the town clerk took advantage
Said the borough surveyor
You'll have to pay her
You've totally altered her frontage.

We often had to deviate from the river and although Capital Sports' nicely bound route guidebook was very detailed we frequently got lost. It didn't help that the route guide was in miles while our brains had long been programmed to think in kilometres and that our mathematics was not very good. But, whenever we agreed on a certain route Rex was apt to growl in a negative fashion – like a bear that is voiding its tappen. [*A tappen, I discovered, is a plug of pine needles swallowed by a grizzly bear which then blocks its rectum. This stops its bodily functions for several months while it is hibernating. If you are to bump into a grizzly bear in the forest it is best to avoid doing so while it is concentrating on ejecting its tappen. – Ed*] The only way to stop the dissentient growling was to elect him as navigator which we conspired to do. We began calling him Henry, after the 15th century Portuguese explorer, Prince Henry the Navigator. The promotion went to Rex's head and from then on he cycled ahead of the peloton. He pedalled so fast and confidently that we were almost dragged along in his slipstream. Rex was uncannily good at navigating but Richard said that with *my* navigation we saw a great deal more of England. Everybody agreed with him and I felt quite proud and might have coloured a little.

The guidebook might read: 'Exit the hotel and turn left. Turn first left into Weedle Street (0.2km). At T-junction turn right to Lower Piddle-in-the-Marsh (0.6km). Cross main road, pass under bridge to the Fall Inn riverside pub 2.1km) ...' It sounds easy enough but nothing in life is easy and Rex eventually capitulated because he couldn't stand the noise when a controversy arose over his chosen direction. But at least the experience stopped his growling for almost an hour. It must be remembered that Rex already held a position of heavy responsibility – that of Treasurer. He had been Treasurer since 2002. Although we argued with him in his capacity as Navigator nobody would ever have dared argue with him in his capacity as Treasurer in case a snap election swung the responsibility of controlling the kitty in their direction. Rex's word as Keeper of the Kitty was law and we often had to wait till he was in a good mood to ask him how much we were allowed to spend on our next meal. But we learned to ply him with more than his fair share of wine at dinner and so soften him up so that if we wanted port or schnapps after dinner he would release the necessary funds.

We first hit civilisation at the pretty little town of Lechlade where the river becomes navigable to pleasure cruisers. The service centres for these leisure craft are the 17th century wharves from which the Cotswold stone that built London's St Paul's Cathedral was loaded onto barges and taken down stream. By mid-afternoon we entered Clanfield, an agreeable and quiet little town of tall trees and tall Victorian houses whose name means 'clean field' – free of timber. It's a reminder perhaps of the time when the Upper Thames was a canopy forest felled by the Romans and the timber floated down the Thames to Londinium. At the western entrance to the town is the Plough, a majestic wisteria-clad Elizabethan manor of Cotswold stone where we spent the night. Its restaurant is a series of cosy interlinked rooms with flagstone floors polished by five centuries of use. Its restaurant has separate and comprehensive menus for fish and game. We ate with great enthusiasm for it had been a long day. The accommodation chosen for our particular sample of the set piece cycle tour of the Thames Valley was not only comfortable but provided food as good as anywhere we'd experienced across the Channel. Gone are the days when the English considered boiled cabbage a Sunday treat.

Our second night was at the Randolph in Oxford and that evening we sauntered down to Jalals, a popular Indian restaurant which we found filled with merry university students, some sitting with shoes on their heads. (England is funny that way.) We noticed the girls were wearing skirts that in our day were called belts.

The Randolph Hotel is in the middle of the city opposite the Ashmolean Museum which is probably the oldest public museum in the

Western World. We felt a little out of place at the Randolph arriving, as we did, in our cycling kit and being greeted by a top-hatted doorman who, with admirable dignity, showed us where to stow our cycles. Next morning after breakfast we gathered in the foyer, this time feeling very conspicuous in our gaudy cycling clothes among smartly-dressed business people, when Peter, looking as usual the most bizarre of all of us in his black Rasputin-like ensemble, was enthusiastically greeted by an exceptionally well-groomed man with a crocodile-skin briefcase – Robert Lacey, the Queen's biographer. Lacy, a best-selling author and historian, had to introduce himself to Peter and remind him how they had met a few weeks earlier at Davos in Switzerland during the World Economic Forum. We were all impressed that the British Royals' most respected commentator knew Peter but Peter didn't know him.

On our way out of Oxford Mike Dunmore joined us and guided us past some of the 39 colleges and into the quadrangle of one of the world's greatest libraries, the 600-year-old Bodleian with its 2.5 million books – including, let it be said, two or three of my own. It's almost a state library and it is entitled to a free copy of every book published in Britain. Sadly, we had no time to browse.

Mike showed us the Eagle and Child pub – the 'Bird and Baby' as it is known – where, from 1939 until 1962, writers such as CS Lewis and JR Tolkien used to meet – members of The Inklings who read to each other from their own works, seeking criticism and ideas.

The Queen was visiting the city that morning so there was the smell of fresh paint. That's the English – as soon as they hear the Queen is arriving they quickly paint everything and then line the pavements waving little flags and smelling of paint and turps. Peter said, 'It's all the Queen smells – fresh paint, wherever she goes.' At dinner one night he told us of the couple of times he had met the Queen and said at their first meeting that she smelled of disinfectant. Journalists like to square up to each other, toe-to-toe, when it comes to name-dropping, though, on tours, we older journalists never do. Well hardly ever. In any event I am usually knocked out during the first round in name-dropping jousts but on this occasion I mentioned, once again, my own meeting with royalty when I met Prince Charles at Powys Castle in Wales and how before the meeting I had been handed a note saying what I could and could not do: such as

I couldn't ask the Prince a question – a rule that I swept aside by saying, 'How d'you do, Sir?' The note also advised me to go the lavatory before the meeting (there would be no facilities in the garden where we were meeting). I did as commanded and was in two minds whether to reassure Charles that I had washed my hands afterwards.

At the time – and this was soon after South Africa adopted a universal franchise – a number of British royals had begun visiting our new and, once-again respected country, and I thought it a good idea to use my newspaper column in *The Star* to appraise readers of how to behave when meeting royalty. I sought advice from my friend, Lt-Col Sir John Chamberlayne-Arbuthnot, Bt, CVO, BC, ASAP, CNA, AA, an expert on protocol and one who is never in doubt about which way up to hold his fork when eating peas.

'Potty,' I said (the nickname Potty is short for 'chamber pot' which, of course, is derived from the *Chamber*layne part of his name), 'Potty, as you know, Her Majesty, Queen Elizabeth II and His Royal Highness, Prince Philip the Duke of Edinburgh, are coming to South Africa. It occurs to me that a lot of my readers – being so well-connected as indeed they are – could suddenly be confronted by a Royal Personage and they would probably appreciate advice about how to conduct themselves.' As I say, Potty knows which way to pass the port so his advice is useful and it boiled down to this:

Shaking hands: You may take the Queen's hand only if she offers it. Do not kiss it (especially if you have been eating savouries topped with cheese whorl); do not hang on to it, or wring it, or shake it vigorously.

Bowing and scraping: Gentlemen should bow ever so slightly. To perform a deep bow when the Queen is not expecting it could mean your forehead coming to rest on the Royal Bosom or your face becoming buried in her bouquet which could induce a hay-fever attack, causing you to sneeze all over her.

Ladies may curtsy, but those with arthritic knees should not attempt this unless they can do it without knee-clicks and gasps, and they must be sure they can straighten out their legs within a reasonable time – say less than five minutes.

Pleasantries: Don't bother to introduce yourself unless the Queen introduces herself first. If she says something like 'How do you do? I'm the Queen of England' you may respond by saying, 'How do you do? I am Bert Anderson' if indeed that is your name.

Don't take the question 'How do you do?' literally. Don't, for instance, go into details about your colon. She is unlikely to be really interested in how you do do.

Conversing: NEVER ask the Queen a question. If she asks you about your children do not take this as an invitation to say: 'They're fine, how's Charles getting along with the Rottweiler?' Never make personal observations such as 'You don't look at all like you do on the stamps.'

If the Queen asks you a question, answer it in as few words as possible – she probably has 200 other guests to speak to in the next three minutes.

If she asks you what you do for a living, don't thrust your hands into your pockets and lean against a pillar and tell her how you travel in bathroom ware and that if ever she needs to fix a drip you'd give her a special price. She might think you're referring to somebody in the family.

Physical contact: Never touch the Queen's person. Apart from briefly shaking her hand – if she proffers it – never put your hand on her shoulder or pat her cheek or fiddle with her jewellery, asking how much it cost.

Prince Philip: With Prince Philip you can relax a little, but do not take too much advantage of his affability should he be displaying any that day. If he calls you by your first name do not presume to call him Phil.

Greetings: Do not greet Royal Personages unless you are greeted first. If you see Prince Philip coming out of the gents it is polite to ignore him. Do not resort to wisecracks like 'Did you remember to wash your hands?'

Taboo words and expressions: Howzit? Nickers. Sweetie. Charlieboy. Hey? Lavatory. Andrew. Money. Fergie. You. Income tax. Bloody hell. Will you give me a hand to change my car oil?

The ups and downs

Halfway along the Thames we reached the small town of Dorchester whose High Street – now, sadly, a busy through road – passes between half-timbered houses. This is where, after three solid and tiring hours of cycling along the bumpy Thames Path, we stopped for lunch at a half-timbered coaching house called The George. We parked our bikes in a yard largely unchanged since the days when stage coaches parked overnight and the steaming horses were groomed.

Our route-book advised, 'Don't miss the Abbey tea rooms.' We did. We also missed the late-Norman abbey, said to be one of the most imposing buildings in the Thames Valley. We missed such a lot. It made us realise the route we were taking deserved two weeks.

It began to rain a little as we entered the picture-book scenery around Pangbourne where Kenneth Grahame lived and where he wrote *The Wind in the Willows* and where Jerome K Jerome of *Three Men in a Boat* stayed at The Swan with his two companions (not forgetting the dog) but it did not rain enough for us to use our rain gear.

The English call a lot of their hills 'downs'. The Marlborough Downs and the Berkshire Downs, for example. Both were just off route. Downs: how gentle they sound. But it would be more honest to call them 'ups' because for every three minutes of shouting with ecstasy while freewheeling *down* a hill means 20 minutes grunting *up* the other side. On the fourth day we came into abrupt collision with the Chiltern Hills. Nobody had told us about them. In fact the English slyly avoid the term 'hills'. They simply say 'the Chilterns' or 'the Cotswolds' or just 'the downs'.

English cyclist: 'I say, let's visit the Chilterns today!'

South African: 'Ja man, they sound like nice people, hey?'

In fact the Chilterns were so steep it was tough enough walking up them. Even Richard was forced to walk but only because his gears slipped and he lost 'cadence'. (Cadence? Don't ask me.) A downhill should logically have followed but all I recall was another near-vertical ascent. The knowledgeable reader might scoff and say that the Chilterns rise to only 260m above sea level and that we have rugby players taller than that. [*There readers go again! – Ed*] Nevertheless the climb was the most severe in my experience. On the other hand there were no serious hills before the Chilterns and the only ones after that were the molehills which sometimes make the going bumpy along the Thames Path where it traverses meadows which it so often does.

It had been a strange day from the beginning. We had cycled along a narrow, undulating track with some awkward corners through a beautiful broadleaf forest and then we had to push our bikes up some very steep and long steps. As we emerged and regrouped a young woman jogged past. Jogged? No, she was running as if the winter sales had started without her. We overtook her on the flat and then she overtook us on a hill and, so help me, she disappeared from sight and only ten minutes later did we almost catch up with her. We decided she must have been an Olympic runner.

A few kilometres on we rode for some time through a vast country estate some of whose paddocks contained South American alpacas (related to the llama and bred for their lightweight wool) and some contained blanketed thoroughbreds. Many nearby fields were growing opium – hectare upon hectare of it – for the pharmaceutical industry.

Late one afternoon we became happily lost in the warm flat countryside but somehow found the Perch and Pike, our delightfully cosy B&B at South Stoke. Here Alan's son, Giles Calenborne, a computer boffin who worked nearby, joined us for dinner with his wife, Lauren, their small son and their month-old twins. We were impressed to hear that the diminutive Lauren had often cycled The Argus and run the 75km Comrades Marathon, one of the toughest marathons in the world. Noticing that we were pretty tired she asked Rex, as one athlete to another, how many kilometres he'd covered that day. Rex took a long time answering and then said how beautiful the twins were.

As we neared London we encountered more and more commuter towns – leafy streets, elegant houses and fine schools such as Radley College with its vast playing fields and magnificent golf course. The boys strode purposefully hither and thither in flowing academic gowns like extras in a Harry Potter film.

One night we slept over at Eton but, just before the town, we took a wrong turn and found ourselves, illegally, on a 120km/h motorway at peak hour. It was a terrifying experience, being passed at arm's length by reticulated 30-ton trucks. We pedalled so fast our feet were just a blur. Once we were clear of the freeway we found ourselves cycling down a deserted street between Eton's 600-year-old school (which has all the outward charm of a Victorian prison) and its legendary playing fields where Wellington played and where,

151

it is said, the Battle of Waterloo was won. We arrived late and exhausted at Eton and once again were sorry not to have had the time to visit the school among so many other places. Just across the ancient Thames Bridge was the world's largest inhabited castle. That too we would be unable to visit.

The road to London

Early on a sunny Sunday morning we crossed the Eton-Windsor Bridge and rode past 1 000-year-old Windsor Castle. The Royal Standard was not flying so we knew Peter's friend was absent – although Peter confided she sometimes flies the flag even when she is not there, just to fool the burglars. (It is amazing what one learns when travelling with a bunch of seasoned journalists.)

For the next few hours our route followed the Thames Path except at Staines where, I think, we must have taken a wrong turn for we ended up pedalling through the town and past a big school just as the children were pouring out. As I puffed my way up the hill, well behind the peloton, a schoolgirl shouted, 'Go for it Grandpa! You can do it!' Knowing how neurotic the Brits are about striking a child I refrained from hitting her on the head with my bicycle pump.

We passed Runnymede where the Magna Carta was sealed in 1215; past Hampton Court, scene of so many royal dramas; past the former royal hunting grounds on Richmond Common and then Kew Gardens. Being Sunday and sunny the Thames Path was busy and we had to thread our way through throngs of people, a few on bikes but most of them on foot.

If the truth be told we were all a little nervous about cycling to the heart of London where our B&B was. We stopped reading the instruction manual and simply followed the river's right bank, keeping to the main road until we reached Hammersmith Bridge which we crossed. Once we were on the left bank London suddenly became very serious – a maze of little roads as well as busy junctions. The problem was that from Kew the manual had an instruction for every two or three hundred metres and it became a bit like being on a paper chase in the middle of the Battle of Waterloo. To stick to the instructions would mean stopping and probably arguing at very frequent intervals. To quote directly from the guide book:

152

At the end of the alleyway you finally leave the Thames and **turn immediately left** *towards the busy road and take the ramp down to cross underneath the Hammersmith Road.*

At the far side of the tunnel **turn left** *at the top of the ramp and* **turn right** *almost immediately onto a path SP (signpost) Ravenscourt Park.*

Straight ahead into Cromwell Avenue.

At the junction with King Street **turn right and second left** *into Studland Road.*

Under the railway bridge and follow the road as it bends right.

Turn left *into Lamington Street*

It would have been fine and very interesting had it been early on a weekend morning before the traffic build-up for the route was designed to take one through parks, along cycle tracks and through quiet streets. But to have followed it would have meant reading out loud no fewer than 41 instructions over the next 6km. Richard who, as usual, was some way ahead, was shouting above the din of traffic, 'We're in Kensington High Street – let's carry on straight into London!' It was a sensible idea for we were pretty tired. We soon reached Kensington Gardens and briefly admired Britain's most unrestrained monument – the freshly gilded, steeple-shaped, lavishly ornamented Albert Memorial – poor Queen Victoria's tribute to her dead Prince Consort. Whenever I see it I am reminded of how the Goon Show once blasted it off to the Moon. We badly disrupted the flow of traffic around Hyde Park Corner and then cycled down Constitution Hill past Green Park where I recalled an episode when Queen Victoria mused about incorporating Green Park into Buckingham Palace grounds. She asked Prime Minister Disraeli what it would cost her. He said, 'Your crown, Ma'am.'

Then we cycled up the pink-surfaced mall and, eventually, round crowded Trafalgar Square. On any given day there are rarely fewer than a million visitors in central London yet, miraculously, one sees no traffic-flattened people. Indeed, as soon as one shows an inclination to cross a street the stream of traffic stops and, even if the street is six lanes wide, the traffic parts like the Red Sea did for Moses.

Nevertheless we were intimidated by the streams of double-decker buses and the cabs that scurry around London like whirligig beetles and so we took to slowly cycling along the pavements. I learned later that cycling on pavements is a matter of heated controversy in the newspapers. Pedestrians protest bitterly. But while no pedestrians have been killed by cyclists, of the 130 cyclists killed annually on the roads, half resulted from pedestrians blundering into them and knocking them into the traffic stream. Apart from pedestrians not wanting cyclists on pavements many motorists feel they shouldn't be using the roads either – because they don't pay road tax and their numbers are increasing. As we cautiously threaded our way along Whitehall some pedestrians loudly objected and one threatened to punch Rex. It was just as well we all missed the altercation because, as one, we would have leapt to his defence (for he had the kitty) and we would probably have triggered riots clean across London.

Inevitably we became scattered and I crossed Westminster Bridge alone though I could pick out somebody's white shirt passing the Houses of Parliament. Miraculously, within the space of five minutes, we all arrived outside our hotel with its very forgettable name – Hotel Premier Travel Inn – right next to the giant Ferris wheel, the London Eye. The hotel occupies the now converted monstrous pile that was once called County Hall, built to house the London County Council's chambers.

We woke up to a cold and rainy London and left straight after an early breakfast to resume our journey eastwards along the well-paved Thames Path. Our goal was Gravesend 70km away where the river merges with the North Sea. I was amazed at the numbers of other cyclists using the path to go to work – amazed because the London I knew (and, if you'll forgive the phrase) where I was brought up, used to rise late, especially on a wet Monday. Usually only Parliamentarians rise early because in Britain the sleepless have always governed the sleepy.

Across the river St Paul's Cathedral stood well above the damp cityscape. We passed under many famous bridges as well as past the Royal Festival Hall, the National Film Museum, Royal National Theatre, the Tate Modern (gallery) and then under the spidery Millennium Bridge. As a child I remember seeing this entire area ablaze night after night from German bombing. We used to live half a kilometre away until the Clarkes decided to move to the Midlands where there were fewer bombs falling per square mile. The area was, until the war, the world's busiest port with as many as 1 000 shipping movements a week bringing raw materials from the Empire – including sugar cane – to be processed and sold at a great profit. Today, with the Empire now a distant memory, the obsolete wharves (usefully demolished by German bombing) have been replaced by apartments and offices. The Germans were probably the best town planners the East End ever had, creating much-needed open space.

Every few minutes we passed a building, bridge or site that was worthy of attention – Shakespeare's Globe Theatre, London Bridge, Fishmonger's Hall, Billingsgate Market, HMS *Belfast*, Tower of London and Tower Bridge, the Design Museum, the Clink (the prison whose name passed into the English language), past the Golden Hind (in which Drake circumnavigated the world between 1577 and 1580) and on to Greenwich where we circled the magnificent clipper, the *Cutty Sark*, now landlocked. This, we felt, was the ideal place to have ended the tour for Greenwich is a fascinating place to spend a day. Technically, anyway, the Thames Path ends here and the more utility and much less attractive Sustrans Cycle Route begins.

But we had set out to cycle right to the end of the river and that's where we headed on glistening pavements with four or five hours' cycling ahead of us.

It's an interesting route all the same. There are a few diversions where one can easily become lost and, once or twice, we did just that. Twice we found ourselves weaving among heavy main-road traffic in cycle lanes that followed the gutter and often went over drains while buses and lorries brushed past. Negotiating the rush-hour traffic stream through Woolwich, Peter and I lost the other four, or they lost us. The two of us picked our way back to the Thames side and resumed pedalling beside the gradually widening river whose muddy edges revealed discarded bed frames and other junk exposed by the ebbing tide. After two or three hours' cycling in the rain, passing scrap yards and untidy factory yards, we came to an obstruction and were forced off course into Erith whose name, appropriately, means 'muddy landing place'. Here we stopped at a random pub to gain respite from the rain, wondering how far ahead the other four were. There seemed no chance of seeing them again until we all homed in at our destination. But not many minutes later – and not for the first time on this tour – the others miraculously rocked up at the pub, having spotted our bikes standing outside.

We decided to lunch at the next town, Dartford, where, half a century ago, Harvey worked for a while as a young reporter on the *Kentish Times*. We settled ourselves in the bay window of an inn just outside the central area. We ordered cheese and tomato sandwiches. Sorry, said the waitress, no tomato. Just cheese then. Sorry, no cheese either. We said how about egg and bacon?

No egg or bacon – but they said they'd find something.

Then they came back and said there was no bread.

I think at this stage they felt a bit silly and sent somebody out to buy a loaf. In the event it was an oval loaf and from it they inexpertly made six ham sandwiches of very different sizes depending on which came from the two thin ends of the loaf and which came from the middle.

In the late afternoon, wet, hungry, but triumphant, we arrived in Gravesend.

I could hear the schoolgirl's voice – 'Go for it grandpa! You can do it!'

Well, dammit, we did it.

Chapter Ten

The Thames expedition had, in a sense, been serious stuff. Or, let's say, we had expected it to be. We had expected to have gone much deeper than we did into the layers of the Thames' history for traditionally the river has been the main artery of England's busiest and most innovative and intellectual region. In the event we had left ourselves far too little time to explore its many major historical sites, browse its great museums and libraries and even to enjoy the river. I thought that a change of pace directly afterwards would be a good idea – a hedonistic, unchallenging week of cruising the 'D roads' of France, those quiet capillaries that from the Atlantic to the Mediterranean form a fine mesh across Europe's largest country. I had in mind indulging once again in those epicurean delights, of reassuring the French about the quality of their wines – with a little cycling in between to ease our consciences.

'But we cycled in France only three years ago,' said Rex when I first raised the possibility of going back there.

'Yes, but remember the food – and the wine!'

His eyes crossed and a trace of moisture appeared at the corner of his mouth.

'And that was only in south-western France,' I reminded him. 'To leave it at that is like being at a smorgasbord and only trying one end of the table. Now we must sample it higher up, in western France. Apart from that it will be a sort of private victory lap to mark the end of the fifth *Tour de Farce*.'

The Loire basin downstream from Tours is essentially flat – ideal terrain for coarse cycling. The landscape has been smoothed over by millennia of periodic flooding of the five rivers – the Vienne, Indre, Cher, Loire and Mayenne – that meander into the mainstream Loire once the Loire has turned abruptly west to seek the Atlantic. The area is famous for its splendid wines as well as some extravagant chateaux and pleasant little villages whose folk are forever cooking and where simply everybody wears the *cordon bleu* ribbon and practices *haute cuisine* and all that other jolly old French stuff.

During the train journey I recalled how a reader had suggested in an e-mail that we must be taking performance-enhancing drugs – just like the riders in the *Tour de France*. The reader, Mokati Ramphele, had written: 'Many of us have long been puzzled that a band of men with an average age of 68 can cycle for days across Ireland, England and France quaffing wine and sinking beers without any performance-enhancing substances.' Soon after we returned to South Africa the *Tour de France* drug scandal broke and at the time of writing it is threatening to sink the famous race as surely as that iceberg sank the *Titanic* with Kate Winslet on board. This would leave our *Tour de Farce* as Europe's premier cycling event. My colleagues laughed at the suggestion that we would pop pills like professional cyclists but as my companions began to nod off to the soporific hum of the train I began to think to myself, what if it's true? What if one of us is taking anabolic steroids? It would reduce us to the level of the *Tour de France*. I narrowed the eyes and looked at each of my companions in turn. Obviously it wasn't me. I just take a daily beta-blocker pill, a pill for cholesterol, another for a reason I have forgotten and half an aspirin a day to thin the blood. Nobody can accuse me of pill popping. In any event beta-blockers have the pharmacological action of blocking ones betas, whatever they are, but it slows down the heart and therefore withholds blood from the muscles – the very opposite of performance enhancing.

But, I asked myself, if one of the others is pill popping – the question is who? Or even whom?

Richard! By Jove! It could be him! Why had I never thought of it? I've often wondered how it is that he is always so far in front and how is it that he can carry on a normal conversation while pedalling up a 5km hill? Maybe I should ask Alan, who is his roommate in the event of us having to share rooms, to keep an eye on him. Mind you, Alan is never far from the front ... He will carry on about rugby and cricket for up to an hour come hill or dale. Now, I happen to know he takes pills but, he says, they are anti-inflammatory for his back from when a Douglas fir in the Yukon rolled on him. But I bet that's what all the druggies say in the *Tour de France*.

I considered Peter. Although he's not far off 60 he is forever dashing up and down the line no matter how far strung out it is. And after three tours he *still* has not learned to dodder like the rest of us. Could he pass a urine test? Should I challenge him to? Should I get all my companions to have urine tests?

And there's Harvey, deep in his 70s, who never tires. What's he got that I haven't? Erythropoietin? When he fell off his bike speeding down a hill in Italy, he never mentioned the pain until next day. Anabolic steroids dull pain ... Coincidence?

I looked at Rex. He once gave me a tablet when I had a toothache and it had me shouldering pedestrians aside and vaulting over car bonnets to cross the road. He said he'd used them to relieve the pain during the time he had shingles. But did he really have shingles? Did anybody actually *see* him with shingles? And, come to think of it, his voice often descends into a rumbling growl – a typical sign of a testosterone overdose.

It was disappointing to realise all five of them could be pill popping.

Yet, as Harvey pointed out, bicycles, like any other form of transport, need fuel – and as our stomachs are the bicycle's fuel tank we have to take in substances. A banana or a beer contain performance-enhancing substances. They help one propel a bicycle for several kilometres. Peter said that a banana will propel a bicycle 12.7 kilometres while a poached egg will be good for only 10.2 kilometres. Sometimes, I suspect, Peter makes up these statistics. While the stomach is the fuel tank the legs are its pistons but what is the best fuel to drive those pistons? With the exception of the time Rex subverted us into having a Remy Martin cognac at 10 am in the morning and I found myself powering up a hill as if turbo-charged, we have never reached any satisfactory conclusions regarding bicycle fuel and octane ratings but, undeterred, we continue our experiments. It was, in fact, this line of research that persuaded us, in the name of science, to return to France and retest their wines and cognacs after our ride down the Thames.

Cycling for Sissies

We were in high spirits as the TGV slid silently out of Paris' Montmartre Station en route to the Loire Valley. Peter was telling us about the time when, in 1988, he had taught the Prime Minister of France, Michel Rocard, how to toyi-toyi and how he had dined at the Hotel Matignon, the French prime minister's Paris residence, as the guest of Mme Mitterand with the future South African president, Thabo Mbeki.

At Tours we changed trains for Chinon on the Vienne where our bicycles were waiting for us.

In warm midday sunshine we dragged our wheeled luggage from the station and down a long tree-lined street towards midtown. Chinon is only two streets wide – one along the river and the other running parallel – and which was so quiet we were able to walk down the middle of it. We sounded like a Garrett locomotive as our luggage rumbled behind us and somebody remarked on how amazing it was that we put a man on the Moon before anybody invented wheeled luggage.

We had, once again, called upon the patience and organising ability of Serena Cartwright in Cape Town to organise our Loire ride. Serena helped organise our first ride in France and, the following year, our ride in Italy. She represents an organisation called Cycling for Softies based in Manchester that specialises in cycling in France. It is run by Susi Madron and 2006 was the organisation's silver jubilee year. As I mentioned earlier, one or two of my companions had bristled a bit when I told them Cycling for Softies was organising our tour – after all we are a rugged bunch: two were, in their younger years, serious rugby players; another had, not long before, climbed Kilimanjaro; another sailed in the Cape-to-Rio yacht race – even I (cough, cough) had summited Sandton's 100m-high Lone Hill kopje by the difficult eastern face with all its burrs that stick to one's socks.

160

Rex kept calling it 'Cycling for Sissies'. As it turned out, Cycling for Softies was just what we needed.

Chinon's main square is dominated by a twice-life-size statue of Joan of Arc in full body armour and in full cry riding a plunging steed, nostrils flared like a rocking horse, and her one-ton sword pointing across the Vienne where once the dreaded English provocatively twirled their moustaches. The English kings at the time ruled from Scotland to the Pyrenees and occupied two thirds of France. I thought the statue reminiscent of a Harley Davidson rider going over a cliff. The significance of the dramatic statue is that it was in Chinon, in 1429, that 17-year-old Jeanne d'Arc managed to obtain an audience with the Dauphin – the future King Charles VII of France. It was halfway through the Hundred Years War which, as noted before (please find) went into extra time – 116 years to be exact. Joan, the daughter of a ploughman, told Charles of a vision she had experienced which revealed that France would defeat their English oppressors on the battlefield. Charles believed her and, led by Joan, went into battle and the French won. But during the second half of the war the English routed the French and the English Church set up a court that declared Joan, by now a prisoner, a heretic and sentenced her to burn at the stake in Rouen. In fact the fire was lit away from the stake and the 19-year-old was slowly roasted in the hope she would repent. She never did. (It is difficult to know what Christ would have made of Christians in those days – or even today, come to think of it.) Joan, France's major saint, was declared a saint only in 1920. The long walls and turrets of the castle where she met Charles dominate Chinon.

The weather was perfect throughout our week of cycling and the scenery was gentle and tranquil with lots of deep beech woods, open fields with young crops, vineyards, delightful little towns often with open-air markets selling fat strawberries, shining vegetables, magnificent cheeses and fresh fish.

As we were cycling along I wondered about all the work that goes into organising a tour for six and what I get out of it – especially since I lost the job of Treasurer when I was getting quite a lot out of it. I supposed it's the companionship and the exercise and the chance to explore. I think that's what we all want. We are all very different people. Alan tends to be quiet unless the conversation is about rugby or cricket. It's a pity Jake White can't listen into the conversations between Alan and Richard on the subject of rugby. The selectors too would at least know what to do. Alan gets frequent calls on his cell phone from his sons, Wade in South Africa and Giles in the Thames Valley, who keep him informed about such vital matters as the cricket score or the make-up of the team to play the All Blacks. As I said earlier, Richard spends most of the time in front – sometimes far in front for he can cycle three times the distance we cover. Alan and Harvey are never far behind. Rex, no doubt because of his thrice-weekly golf is much more fit than I and tends to cycle at an even pace, in silence, in fourth position. Peter alternately races up and down the line but often deliberately falls back to keep me company. He is forever talking and might, while we are riding in a tight peloton on the flat, suddenly ask us to guess how many cars, let's say, the BMW factory produces each month.

'Seventeen and a half,' I might suggest just as a point of departure.

'Ten million,' somebody else will say.

'456 976,' offers a third person.

'Thirty-six thousand!' he will say. (I'm making the figure up. Sometimes I think he is too.)

'Really?' somebody will say.

One day he said, 'How many Blue Trains are there?' The Blue Train is the famous super-luxury train that plies between Pretoria and Cape Town. I have always thought there was only one.

'8 769!' somebody says.

'No ...'

'21 878?'

'No. There are nine,' Peter will say. 'Now guess how many Bullet Trains there are in Japan.'

We all guess wildly.

'There are 278,' he will say (again I forget the number).

I asked him once why he quizzes people instead of coming right out and say, 'Did you know there are 327 ways of lacing up your shoes?' He said it is because journalists would answer, 'Yes, of course, I knew that' or they'd say, 'I always thought it was about that number' when, in fact, they hadn't the foggiest idea.

162

He's right. Journalists will never admit that there is something they don't know. Some years ago Robert Richardson of *The Independent* in London had a go at leader writers – who are the worst know-alls of all – in a humorous series titled 'media types'. A leader writer, I should perhaps explain, is a person who writes 'editorials' or 'leaders' in newspapers. These are traditionally short and anonymous, wrote Richardson – meaning (he explained) the editorials. Their words reflect the considered opinion of the newspaper. Leader writers, when in company, say things like, 'I must put you right on that point.'

Five of the six of us were former leader writers. I still write the occasional one. As Richardson pointed out, 'It's a funny way to earn a living even allowing for the fact that journalism is no profession for grown-ups.' Leader writers, he said, have a permanent licence to pontificate.

He says they betray themselves in their opening words and he gives this example: 'Until yesterday few people had heard of Zemogogul ...' 'This includes the leader writer who only became aware of its existence at morning conference. Since then he has found out (a) where it is; (b) how to spell its president's name; (c) its GDP; and (d) vaguely what is happening there. He will now tell Zemogogul exactly how it should conduct its affairs.'

As a leader writer for 25 years I take issue with Richardson. Leader writers sweat like foundry workers over their jobs. On a good day it may take up to 15 minutes to sort out a tricky international situation and give world leaders the guidance they need. National affairs can take up ten minutes and longer. Local affairs can take a minute and a half unless – as it did in my day – it involves, say, some constitutional complication in the Metropolitan Chamber's interim strategic framework, in which case it can take up to two minutes.

On the strength of Richardson's remarks I devised some 'shortcut keys' so that if a leader writer is uncertain about what advice to give, let's say, to President Thabo Mbeki, he (leader writers are invariably 'he' because females talk too much and are altogether too practical) has a button on his word processor marked OTOH. This automatically types the words 'on the other hand', a phrase which, Richardson points out, is a leader writer's favourite. Thus the first half of his editorial will spell out what Mbeki should do and the second half, beginning with 'on the other hand', will say the opposite. Then, when things go wrong and Mbeki finds himself in early retirement in Port Alfred playing Bingo with old ladies, the leader writer can say 'we told you so'. Except you won't find a WTYS button on a leader writer's word processor because he would never use so crass a phrase. Instead, twirling his pointy finger in the air, he will home it in on a button inscribed AWSO – 'as we said on ...' and simply fill in the date. Another well-worn and shiny button is marked IAWD – 'is a welcome decision', and another is OTWT which means 'only time will tell'. This phrase, said Richardson, indicates the leader writer had an early lunch engagement and no time to arrive at a logical conclusion.

Our second night was spent in Saumur, an interesting and strung-out town along the Loire. Like so many towns in this region it is dominated by an imposing chateau, this one owned by the dukes of Anjou. Our hotel, Anne d'Anjou, was a splendid place overlooking the river which is 400 metres wide at that point and appears to be quite silted with long sandbanks. Like the majority of hotels in which we stayed the Hotel Anne d'Anjou had an elegant restaurant, the Menesterel, and we wondered if it required a tie. But no, smart-casual was sufficient and golf shirts and slacks were fine.

The dinner was nothing short of excellent and we declared Saumur's sparkling Crémant de Loire brut excellent too. In fact we tended from then on to stick mostly to sparkling Saumur wines – *vins mousseux* – for they were light and reasonably priced. I thought they were quite close to the champagne that was produced a little to the northwest and Richard half agreed.

Saumur distinguished itself during World War II when on 10 June 1940, the French government fled Paris, quartering itself in the various chateaux along the Loire Valley. Most of the chateaux were unconnected by phone so to say the government was in disarray would be an understatement. The Germans began bombing the towns to dislodge the French leaders. Winston Churchill flew in hoping to persuade the French to put up a fight. He found nobody in authority. De Gaulle, radioing from London, pleaded with the French to put up some resistance. Alas, they fled even further south – except in Saumur where the École de Cavalerie under Colonel

Daniel Michon with 3 000 cadets held out against 18 000 Germans for three days. The rug was pulled from under them when Marshall Petain made a pact with the Germans and surrendered France. The Germans publicly saluted the courage of the Saumur cadets saying they were the only Frenchmen for whom they could feel any respect. Where was Jeanne d'Arc now that the French really needed her?

Four years later Allied bombing added to the destruction along the Loire until liberating troops moved in. It was hard to imagine anybody dropping bombs on the beautiful and ancient towns along the Loire such as Saumur.

Our third day was spent cruising along country lanes in warm sunshine, deliberately taking a long way round to our next destination. We followed the river for a time before heading away from it and into the hills, pedalling through mixed woodland filled with birdsong and busy with squirrels. One couldn't really get lost even though there were many choices of routes. We spent the entire week cycling on public roads but the driving was considerate. Cycling most of the time in single file, the last person would shout 'Car!' if he heard one approaching. The cry would be taken up down the line until it got to Harvey who might shout, 'What?'

'Car!' everybody would shout with varying degrees of alarm.

'What?' he would repeat.

By then the car would have disappeared and we'd all slide back into our individual reveries.

We became seriously hot and tired by mid-afternoon and were greatly relieved when, in a most delightful piece of countryside with rich fields and voluminous woodlands, we rounded a corner and saw the huge 16th century farmhouse where we were spending the night – Le Vieux Chateau. It was a scattering of ancient stone buildings around an enormous gravel courtyard with a central well. Just beyond was the village of Hommes (pronounced 'um') though the village is almost non-existent. There was more infrastructure on the farm and in its adjacent moated fort than in the entire village. As somebody remarked, 'There's no place like Hommes.'

The proprietor, Mme Hardy, warmly greeted us in perfect English and prepared something approaching a banquet in the baronial dining room furnished with some elegant antiques. We were joined at the long candlelit table by an English couple. The local wines

– beginning with an apéritif of champagne mixed with *cassis* (a blackcurrant liqueur) – had been selected with great thought, not to mention generosity. Peter impressed the English couple no end with his travels with George Soros and having dinner with Peter Ustinov and mentioning what nice company was Helmut Kohl. I told them I'd shaken hands with Prince Charles.

With the knowledge that our cycles were comfortable in Mme Hardy's stables we were able to retire for the night. The double bedroom I shared with Peter was large and, rather sportingly I thought, I offered to take the rather rickety camp bed in the corner while Peter had the enormous double bed. During the night I had to get up and I could not find a light switch. I spent ten minutes in a darkness that was absolute, sliding my hands up and down the walls and becoming more and more desperate. I had forgotten the lights were turned on by hanging cords. I had never known such utter darkness and in the end I had to wake Peter and ask him to turn on his bedside light which he did with good grace. On going back to bed the legs at the head of my bed collapsed and without a light, try as I might, there was nothing I could do to straighten them. Not wanting to wake Peter a second time I tried to sleep with my legs in the air but with all the blood rushing to the brain it became very active like a pot boiling over and I could not sleep. I then decided to remake my bed the other way round so that my feet were lower than my head and spent the night sliding to the floor. I am normally an early riser, rarely staying in bed after 5 am, and this turned out to be the longest night I have known. It simply never got light. So completely dark was it that I assumed dawn must still be some way off. Only when Peter roused me from a brief period of merciful unconsciousness at 8.15 did I discover that he had closed the shutters over the windows – hence the impenetrable darkness. I am normally thinking about lunch by 8.15.

Our ride to Langeais next day (36km) was so short we were there by mid-morning, well before our luggage. We decided to do a 30km detour to visit Villandry's famous garden – hectares of horticultural geometry – a symmetrical patchwork of precisely designed flower and vegetable beds. Even the cabbage patch was as geometrical as a chessboard. I couldn't help wondering how the regimented vegetables were utilised because the removal of just one cabbage for dinner would wreck the whole symmetry. I surmised that the castle owner, Henri Carvallo, popped out to the shops whenever he needed a cabbage.

In contrast to the Villandry Gardens and the many other Renaissance-style gardens one sees around France, there is otherwise a total lack of ostentation in French homes and gardens. Rich or otherwise, Frenchmen build homes that are plain and grow gardens that are at best utility, often with vegetables in their front gardens.

We covered the 15km back into Langeais in much less than an hour – me in the lead the entire way; well, at least until we hit town where, carried away by it all, I took a wrong turn and came in last.

A travel guidebook described Langeais as 'insipid'. We found it quite the opposite. A splendid medieval chateau dominates the middle of town and in its shadow was our very friendly B&B, the Hotel Errard Hosten. It was small and laid back but had seven chefs and a very elegant dining room. We dressed as smartly as we could for dinner – though without ties – and Harvey managed to find a nicely ironed formal white shirt whose elegance was spoiled somewhat by the words 'Save the Whales' which showed through from a t-shirt he was using as a vest. We began with langoustine bisque followed by guinea fowl and *crème brulée* with a Chinon red which, after awaiting Richard's concurrence, we were able to unanimously declare 'excellent'.

The day of our departure from Langeais happened to be market day and from my room at dawn I watched 100 stalls being rapidly assembled in the square. Before we left town we spent a happy hour wandering around it looking at the astonishing variety and quality of the fruit and vegetables, admiring the fish stalls – fresh water and sea fish – and soft goods and wondering why South African cities have nothing comparable. I recognised some of the stalls and the people behind them from a market we had visited two days before and 100km away.

We ended our week back in Chinon and at a charming hotel named the Diderot whose garden was a horticultural delight. There we shared a couple of bottles of Chinon wine with Raymond, a lecturer in French at Bristol University who is also a representative of Cycling for Softies. He had flown in to meet us for we were, apparently, the first of the season's cyclists. He said that although we

167

had enjoyed perfect weather May was usually a bit of a gamble. Our conversation drifted towards what we had learned about coarse cycling in the five years of the *Tours de Farce*. Rex, who at the outset, in 2002, said the whole idea of a retired editor (who hadn't cycled since he was 14) cycling around Europe was 'insane and ludicrous in the extreme' felt that our experiences had borne him out. 'Certainly riding a bike makes me feel younger,' he said, 'but getting off it makes me feel older. Starting up again each day makes me long for death.'

'Trusting the sense of direction of your fellow cyclists might promote fellowship but it always leads to a longer journey.'

But what about the companionship and the spirited debates over a well-earned beer?

'There are easier ways of earning a beer,' he said.

Richard, rather pointedly, said, 'We have certainly learned from our leader' – (here I coughed a little and stared modestly at the ground) – 'that we should never forget maps and a compass and a note of the towns and hotels at which we are staying and ...' (here the junior barrister began speaking – in fact, had he been wearing a lawyer's gown, he would have gripped the shoulder smocking) 'he should have compiled a list for his team regarding essential items needed for our expeditions.

'But if you are follower – as opposed to a leader – then take not only those things (because the leader will forget them) but also sun block, lip ice, money to buy the leader drinks, cell phones for ringing home to find out where we are going, camera, ear plugs (in case you get roomed with a snorer) ...'

His list went on and on until I thought he'd suggest one should take along a framed picture of one's wife to prop up against one's tooth mug at night. As an afterthought, he said, 'Just remember to travel light!'

Harvey, surprisingly, said, 'Don't wear a helmet unless you are absolutely forced to. Helmets are inclined to go to cyclists' heads and make them think they can come down every mountain pass at 150km/h. If you really want to wear a helmet, put it on when you sense you are about to fall.

'It is "a scientific fact" – I read it in *The Telegraph* in London – that cyclists in helmets get knocked down by trucks more often than the bare-headed riders because unhelmeted cyclists win a grain of sympathy. The survey showed that drivers think cyclists in helmets are smart-asses who can cope with heavy traffic brushing their handlebars.

'Wear *two* pairs of Lycra shorts, the inner pair unpadded. This reduces by 50 percent friction on vital parts. (It's the same principle for hikers' socks.)

'Ensure you use a tried-and-tested cycle-hiring company. You are not merely hiring a bike, you are employing a professional who guarantees weeks of riding without mechanical breakdown; who has devised and tested a route to suit you; who has carefully selected your nightly accommodation and possibly your best choice of restaurant. Select your agent as carefully as you choose your companions.'

Cycling gloves are useful too – in case one falls off one's bike. One's hands are usually the first part of the anatomy to hit the deck and gloves protect them. A friend – a professional cyclist – fell off her bike on a tour and badly grazed her palms which made gripping the handlebars extremely painful.

We also learned that wearing a brightly-coloured cycling shirt not only made one highly visible on the road which is a good thing for those who prefer not to be run over by transcontinental juggernauts, but they are easily washed and they dry overnight.

It is sensible to take sun block, though I never do – and eau de Cologne as a disinfectant to be rubbed on one's backside around midday to prevent saddle sores. Harvey said, 'Never put eau de Cologne on your bum unless you are spending a night in gay Paris.'

May and early June are the best months because the weather has warmed up. Even April can be pleasant. Those three out-of-season months (barring Easter) offer not only cheaper prices but quieter roads and amenities.

We had a farewell scotch with Raymond before leaping aboard our bicycles and setting off for our last dinner which entailed a 2km ride, much of it over cobbles. We were booked into a restaurant towards the end of Chinon under the shadow of the fateful Dauphin's castle. Rex, who came up behind us, said he was alarmed at the erratic way we negotiated the narrow roads which, thankfully, were empty. Riding back to the hotel we were *all* alarmed – and even more erratic. We had spent the dinner arguing about where next year's *Tour de Farce* would take place. One said Chile, another Spain, a third said Croatia and Peter was adamant about South Korea. Greece was also suggested.

It was as near a consensus as we'd ever had.

[*This astonishing conclusion is fairly close to the truth. And I mention it only because editors must have the last word. – Ed*]

Travel Consultants

Our consultants regarding routes and bookings were:

Danube (Germany, Austria, Hungary)
Dr Peet du Toit of Duto/Bike and Hike: tel 012 460 8382;
fax 012 460 1843; e-mail duto@za.amadeus.net.
Inge Dobihal, Austria Connection: tel/fax 011 476 3967;
e-mail austria.co@mweb.co.za

Southwest France
For the Canal du Midi – Serena Cartwright (agent for Cycling for Softies
in UK): e-mail cart@hbic.co.za; fax 021 790 2207.
Henry & Christine Stucke of the Auberge Darnis: www.darnis.co.za.
General information: Pierre Saliba, Maison de la France:
tel 011 880 8062; e-mail mdfsa@frenchdoor.co.za

Italy
Serena Cartwright (as above)

Ireland
Tourism Ireland (Helen Fraser): tel 011 339 4865;
e-mail helenf@dpgsa.co.za

Thames Valley
Wendy Carter, Capital Sport, The Red House, Aston Clinton,
Bucks HP22 5EZ, United Kingdom: e-mail wendy@capital-sport.co.uk;
website www.capital-sport.co.uk, tel +44 1296 631671;
fax +44 1296 631703.
VisitBritain (Edwin Swan): tel 011 325 0343; fax 011 325 0344;
e-mail edwin.swan@visitbritain.org

Loire Valley
Serena Cartwright (as above)